Maybe Today

Sermons For Sundays In Advent, Christmas, And Epiphany

Scott Suskovic

CSS Publishing Company, Inc., Lima, Ohio

MAYBE TODAY

For more information about CSS Publishing Company resources, visit our website at www.csspub.com or e-mail us at custserv@csspub.com or call (800) 241-4056.

Cover design by Barbara Spencer

ISSN: 1937-1454

ISBN-13: 978-0-7880-2591-4
ISBN-10: 0-7880-2591-0

PRINTED IN USA

Table Of Contents

**Sermons For Sundays
In Advent, Christmas, And Epiphany**

Maybe Today

Sermons For Sundays In Advent, Christmas, And Epiphany

Scott Suskovic

Editor's Note: Many of these sermons were written as they were to be delivered. Therefore, many contain incomplete sentences. In order that the integrity of the sermon remains true, the sentence structures have not been changed.

— R. K. Allen, Managing Editor

Spiritual Gifts:
God's Gift Of Fulfillment

Now you have every spiritual gift you need.
— 1 Corinthians 1:7 (NLT)

One day all the animals in the forest got together and decided life was not fair. Some animals were better at flying than others. Some animals were better at climbing than others. Some animals were better at swimming than others. To even out the scales, they decided to open a school where the animals could improve in the areas of their weaknesses.

After a month in the program, both tempers and frustration levels were rising. The rabbit was the fastest runner but failed miserably at climbing.

The squirrel was the first one up the tree but never mastered swimming.

The duck could swim for hours but lost every race in the 100-yard dash.

The eagle won all the awards for flying but didn't even enter into the water or attempt to climb the tree.

They were all miserable because they were all forced into a position that did not match their gifts. Instead of celebrating what they enjoyed most and did well, they focused on where they came up short.

Are you mismatched?

Today, 50% of all workers hate their job, 30% endure their job, and only 20% say that they enjoy their job. Why? The same reason the animals in the forest were miserable. There is a mismatch between their work and their gifts.

9

In 1 Corinthians 1 Paul writes to the young Christians, "... you have every spiritual gift you need as you eagerly await for the return of our Lord Jesus Christ ... he is the one who invited you into this wonderful friendship...." Paul writes here as he does in 1 Corinthians 12, Romans 12, Ephesians 4, and elsewhere that the key to living a life of fulfillment is to discover, develop, and use your spiritual gifts.

First Timothy 4:14 says, "Don't neglect the spiritual gift that is in you." Peter Drucker, the father of modern management, was once asked, "What advice would you give to young people who are trying to get ready for the twenty-first century?" Drucker said, "Know your strengths. The most important thing is to know what you're good at. Very few people know that. All of us know what we're not good at. But the reason why so few of us know what we're good at is that it comes so easily. You sweat over what's hard to do. So knowing what you're good at is the first thing you need to know."

Do you know what you are good at? Sometimes other people tell you. Sometimes you take an aptitude test. Most of the time you have to figure it out by trial and error.

In my first church, I helped out with vacation Bible school one summer. Since they were having difficulty recruiting volunteers, I told them to put me anywhere there was an opening. I was placed with fifth-grade girls. I was great with the games. I was an expert at the Bible study. The four chords I can play on the guitar were a hit during music. But when it was time for arts and crafts, I was a mismatch. These fifth-grade girls lived for arts and crafts. That was their favorite part of VBS. We were to make stained glass by gluing tissue paper carefully into pretty patterns on a framed piece of glass. I gave instructions on how to do this project and encouragement along the way, but these stained-glass pictures looked awful. The girls were very polite but kept on saying, "I don't think this is right." I said, "Of course, it is. Just glue the tissue to the glass." But even I knew something was wrong.

I didn't understand the problem until one of the girls said, "Can I read the directions?" When she read, "Glue the tissue paper to the glass," she said, "We don't have tissue paper." I told her, "Yes, we do. I bought you all a box of pastels." She said, "That's not tissue paper you bought. That is Kleenex!" "Is there a difference between tissue and Kleenex?" I asked. Their laughter convinced me of two things. First, there is a difference and second my spiritual gift is not arts and crafts. (And I'm okay with that!)

As you find your spiritual gift, you might have to start by deciding what you are not good at. Just ask a fifth grader for help if you can't figure it out.

Second Timothy 1:6 says, "Fan into flame the gift God gave you." Most of the time, the gifts that we receive are in their raw form. They have to be developed through practice much like fanning a flame into a roaring blaze.

I had a guitar teacher once who was excellent at the guitar. He would spend five hours a day practicing. I neither had the talent, the time, nor the commitment to play that well. After one rather ego-deflating lesson, I asked my teacher if playing the guitar was a God-given gift or did you have to practice five hours a day to get good? I loved his answer. He said, "I think it is a God-given gift ... to be able to practice five hours a day."

Through 1 Corinthians, Paul wrote about living this full, rich life in the Spirit. Beginning with this first chapter, this life is tied into spiritual gifts. The most difficult challenge is to discover your spiritual gift. After that, it needs a lot of work to develop. It comes to us raw. It's up to us to draw it out and perfect it. However, to stop there would miss the point of spiritual gifts. They are to be used, not for your own glory and admiration, but for God's.

In 1 Corinthians 12:6-7 Paul writes, "There are different ways God works in our lives, but it is the same God who does the work through all of us. A spiritual gift is given to each of us as a means of helping the entire church." And in 1 Peter, "God has given gifts to each of you from his great variety of spiritual gifts. Manage them well so that God's generosity can flow through you" (1 Peter 4:10 NLT).

In Matthew 25, Jesus told the story of the master who left on a long journey, leaving his three servants in charge of his wealth. To one he gave five talents, to the other three talents, and to the third, one talent. You know the rest of the story. The first two doubled their talents while the third one wasted his only talent by burying it in the ground and not putting it to use. The first two were rewarded when the master returned. "Well done, good and faithful servant." The third was scolded and punished.

Life is unfair. It is even more unbalanced than in the forest with all the animals. We all don't begin at the same starting point. We all aren't given the same opportunities. We all don't have the same talent. The answer is to discover what spiritual gifts God has bestowed upon you.

Remember the movie *Amadeus*? Amadeus was a pompous, arrogant, impious musician with all the talent. Salieri, on the other hand, was a fine musician — fine enough to know that he wasn't great. Fine enough to know that he didn't have the talent of Amadeus. Fine enough to be driven mad by trying to be Amadeus.

Remember how the story ended? Amadeus died early, wasting his great talent. Salieri ended up in an insane asylum forever comparing himself to Amadeus.

When Paul writes about spiritual gifts, it is a celebration of how God has made you unique. If you are a rabbit, run. Don't spend time trying to climb trees. If you are an eagle, soar. Don't take up swimming lessons. If you are a duck, swim. Forget the 100-yard dash. And be satisfied with these gifts because God has created you to be but one member of the larger body of Christ. Amen.

They Call It Grace

The Lord is not slow about his promise, as some think
of slowness, but is patient with you, not wanting any to
perish, but all to come to repentance. But the day of the
Lord will come like a thief, and then the heavens will
pass away with a loud noise, and the elements will be
dissolved with fire, and the earth and everything that
is done on it will be disclosed. — 2 Peter 3:9-10

What do you hear in Paul's words? Grace or judgment? Law
or gospel? Hope or despair? Advent is a time of waiting. Often we
wonder, "How long? How long can I wait for his coming? How
long can I look off to the horizon? How long can I proclaim his
return?" When we see Paul's words through the filter of grace, we
realize the answer is just a little bit longer.

During a British conference on comparative religions, experts
from around the world debated what, if any, belief was unique to
Christianity. They began with the obvious — the incarnation? The
resurrection? The cross? The debate droned on until C. S. Lewis
wandered into the room and asked, "What's the fuss about?" They
told him that they were discussing Christianity's unique contribu-
tion among the world's religions. Lewis responded, "That's easy.
It's grace."

The notion of God's love coming to us free of charge without
any strings attached seems to go against every human instinct. We
want to get what we deserve. We want things to be fair. So, the
Buddhists have their eightfold path to nirvana, Hinduism has a
doctrine of karma where you get reincarnated over and over again

until you are good enough. The Jews have 613 laws to follow and the Muslims have the five pillars of Islam to obey in order to gain Allah's favor. Each of these religions provides a path that you must follow in order to get to God and get what you deserve. In Christianity, there is no path to God. There is a person who dared to teach, live, die, and rise again to convince a skeptical world that God's grace is enough.

And yet, I dare say, even we Christians have a difficult time accepting grace. We are willing to say that God forgives, but reluctantly — after making the sinner squirm. That's why the story of the prodigal son is so amazing. When the son finally comes to his senses, after squandering the father's money, he returned home destitute, humble, and willing to work as a servant. However, there is no solemn lecture from a stern father with folded arms who says, "I hope you've learned your lesson." Instead, the father humiliates himself by running down the road toward the boy, showering him with a hug, a ring, a robe, shoes, and a party with the fatted calf in his honor. That's grace.

"I don't deserve that, Father." "You are right. You don't. This party is not about you being good enough. It's about my joy to have you home. Now, come and eat."

Grace always comes as a shock to the sinner. We are used to finding a catch or a string attached to every promise. We want to be frugal with God's grace, like the older brother in the story who thought his younger brother didn't deserve a second chance.

Contemporary preacher, Fred Craddock, preached a sermon on the prodigal son but with a twist. Instead of the father honoring the younger, rebellious son, he slipped a ring on the older brother, thanked him for his faithful years of service and killed the fatted calf in honor of doing what was right. And from the back of the sanctuary, a woman yelled out, "That's the way it should have been written."

But it wasn't. That's why Christianity is so unique. It's not written the way we would have written it. Christianity is for the person who feels like the younger son — unworthy, unloved, not good enough. And yet there's a place at the table. It was written for the person who feels like a thief on the cross — out of time, out of luck, out of hope. And yet there is a place at the table. It was written for the person who feels like Judas — my life is a lie; this smile covers the deceit; I've sold my soul to the devil. And yet, Jesus welcomed him to the table. It was written to the person who feels lost, excluded, and forgotten by God and yet, like a lovesick father, God makes sure there is a place at the table. Grace. That's what makes Christianity unique. Jesus came not for the well people but for the sick people, not for the righteous people but for the unrighteous people, not for the good people but for you. "Come and eat."

When Paul wrote about the delay of Jesus' return, it is not to be received with a groan but rather with thanksgiving. This is a God with abundant grace, whose return is delayed in order that more may hear, more may receive, more may believe, and more may be saved. We certainly pray for God to stir up his power and come during this Advent, but I dare say that each one of us knows someone who, if Jesus came today, would not be counted among the saints. God's grace in his delay is for all to believe.

That's what makes Christianity unique — grace. An extravagant grace that overwhelms the people with a place at the table. The delay is for more to be added. And who will be there? Better yet, who deserves to be there? Do you? Of course not, that's the point.

In the Academy of Fine Arts in Venice there hangs a painting by Paolo Veronese that got him into trouble with the church. The painting is Jesus at a banquet with his disciples. That wasn't the problem. But along with them there are some Roman soldiers, a man with a bloody nose, stray dogs, a couple of drunks, dwarfs, black Moors, and even Huns. When called to explain, Veronese said that these were the people whom Jesus probably dined with — the ones whom the religious people thought didn't deserve to be there at the table. Of course they didn't. That's the point. However, the church didn't like the message and made him change the title and make it into a secular scene.

People have a hard time with the thought of Jesus having a party with prostitutes and tax collectors who were received with grace. There is a little elder brother in each one of us who would like Jesus to come today so that those misfits with loose morals would get what they deserve. And we would be rewarded with a place at the table. We don't think the way of grace until we experience it first hand.

Philip Yancey, in his book, *What's So Amazing About Grace*, tells the story of a pastor who was battling with his fifteen-year-old daughter. He knew she was using birth control and on several nights would not bother to come home at all. The parents tried all sorts of punishments but nothing changed — in fact, the more they pushed, the more rebellious she became. The daughter even turned the tables on them and blamed them saying, "It's your fault for being so strict."

The pastor basically said, "I remember standing before the plate-glass window in my living room, staring out into the darkness, waiting for her to come home. I felt such rage. I wanted to be like the father of the prodigal son, and yet I was so furious with my daughter for the way she manipulated us and twisted the knife just to hurt us — and herself. I understood on those nights when the prophets would say that the people wounded God and he cried out in pain."[1]

And yet I must tell you, when *my* daughter finally came home that night, I wanted nothing more than to take her in my arms, to love her, to tell her I wanted the best for her. I was like a helpless, lovesick father who wants above all things to forgive, begin anew and announce with joy, "This my child was dead, and is now alive again. Lost but now found. Bring on the fatted calf. Come and eat."

He knew that the delay of Jesus' return meant that there was hope and grace for his daughter.

Make no mistake. Grace doesn't condone sin and sweep it under the rug with inane excuses such as, "Boys will be boys," "To err is human," "Nobody's perfect," or "Don't be so hard on yourself." Grace is not a free pass to live however you please. Grace, true grace, radical grace is transforming. Luther spent three hours a day in the confessional booth, fasted until near death, slept outside without blankets, and whipped himself to experience the thrashing of Jesus and still couldn't find peace with God. Why? We can never be good enough to earn God's love. That's the problem with the five pillars of Islam and the eightfold path of Buddhism and the 613 laws of

Judaism: Enough is never good enough, not because the path is faulty, but because *I* am faulty. I'm not good enough. The turning point for Luther was grace — a God who loved him, warts and all; a God who came down to Luther because Luther couldn't go up to God; a God who was patient with him; and a God whose grace takes away the rebuke, prepares the table, and welcomes Luther, sinners, prostitutes, bankers, teachers, doctors, lawyers, and even pastors to an extravagant feast. That's grace.

Last month I attended a great funeral, which is a strange way to put it. But what made it great was not the eight granddaughters who sang — though that was sweet, or the nice handout that listed his accomplishments — though that was informative. What made it a great funeral was that the family did not preach him into heaven by saying what a great guy he was. They didn't do a stand-up comedy routine that some people feel compelled to do at funerals. They didn't break down and embarrass themselves or make the congregation uncomfortable. They talked honestly about their father — the good, the bad, and the ugly. What made it a great funeral was that they all knew that Dad had a place at the table — not because he was father of the year or a pillar of the church or a Good Samaritan to the community, but because of grace. Undeserved, extravagant, transforming grace given by God who has not provided us a path we must obey to God but a person — Jesus, who gives you this promise, "You will not get what you deserve, I will not be fair with you, and you are going to hell — over my dead body. You have my word on that." And if that were not enough, he has delayed his coming for one purpose, so that you may hear and believe that this God of grace has a place at the table for you.

"I don't deserve that, Father." You're right. You don't. This delay in his coming is not about you being good enough. It's a gift. It's a gift called grace and it's unique to Christianity. Now, come and eat. Amen.

---

1. Philip Yancey, *What's So Amazing About Grace?* (Grand Rapids, Michigan: Zondervan, 2002).

Advent 3
1 Thessalonians 5:16-24

The Fred Factor

Rejoice always, pray without ceasing, give thanks in
all circumstances; for this is the will of God in Christ
Jesus for you. — 1 Thessalonians 5:16-18

A couple of months ago, I read the book *Good to Great*, in which Gillette was named as a great company. But I was having a hard time getting my mind around what made it so great. Did those executives, engineers, and assembly workers really wake up each morning thinking, "Today is the day that we are going to create an even better razor that will produce smoother legs and faces around the world"? Do people really get charged about that? Am I missing something?

Then a friend gave me a small book called *The Fred Factor*. It reminded me of Paul's words in 1 Thessalonians 5. Paul challenges us to look beyond ourselves, our work, our needs, and our wants to see the bigger picture in how each one of us fits into God's grand design. Paul boils it down to three basic attitude adjustments — rejoice always, pray without ceasing, give thanks in all circumstances.

Fred is a postal worker who has a relationship with the people on his route. They aren't just addresses for Fred. He knows them by name. He protects their mail and watches out for their homes — amazing. He goes the extra mile by establishing relationships and treating people with respect. Have you ever met a Fred? She's that flight attendant on the airplane who can tell a joke while teaching us how to buckle the seatbelt. He's that clerk who finds your

19

wallet, looks you up in the phone book, calls you, and then holds onto your wallet until you return. He's that cable guy who not only installs your cable but sets the timer on your DVD machine that blinks 12:00. Fred probably doesn't wake up in the morning and think, "Today is the day I get to hand out credit card applications, catalogs from Victoria's Secret, and coupon books." That's not it. So what is it? What is that Fred Factor?

It can't be the money that is the motivation. I asked one person about her job and she said, "I design cardboard boxes." I thought, wow, that's a special talent. It's like the engineer who designs those cool envelopes that if you carefully open them on the perforated edges, will then fold into itself and create its own return envelope. Someone smart figured that out. I asked if she went to MIT, to some cardboard design school. "No, it's a boring job. I'm a communications major. For now, this job is a paycheck to cover the bills."

Certainly that's true for all jobs — to pay the bills. But if that's it, we miss Paul's attitude booster to rejoice, pray, and give thanks. If your work is only about a paycheck, there will always be discontent. It will never be enough. Some time ago, Terrell Owens of the Philadelphia Eagles was in a huge battle with the owner of the team because he felt that his 8.1 million dollar contract wasn't enough. He needs 10.5 because, he says, he has a family to support (or was that a small town?). Whenever they say it's not about the money, it's always about the money. Rockefeller was once asked, "How much is enough?" He said, "When I get a little more." Now, be clear here. Money isn't the problem. Working for money isn't wrong. In fact, Jesus said in Luke 10 that the worker deserves his pay. Money isn't a problem. Paul said in 1 Timothy it was, "The love of money was the root of all kinds of evil" (6:10). Why? Because it will never be enough. It will become your god. But I don't think that Fred became a postal carrier for the money.

What else motivates a Fred? Is it his ego? Is Fred like the actress who says, "Mr. Deville, I'm ready for my close up"? Or the professional who really likes that title of doctor, judge, pastor, or vice president of marketing and sales. I remember once hearing an interview with Madonna during her younger, more expressive years in which she was having an argument with a television censor for her lewd acts on stage and she said, "I'm an artist. I need to express myself." Some live and breathe and work for the applause, but not Fred.

Nor was ego the motivation for John the Baptist. He could easily have stolen center stage. He had the crowds, he had the attention, and he baptized Jesus. Yet he kept that ego in check with one simple phrase, "I must decrease. He must increase. I must decrease. He must increase." Paul put it this way, "But all of us who are Christians ... reflect like mirrors the glory of God" (2 Corinthians 3:18). That's what made Fred shine — he wasn't reflecting himself. It wasn't about him. It's not about me.

I heard a great story about an older man who worked for the Wycliffe Bible Translators. He was in maintenance and spent the day repairing motors, fixing leaking sinks, cleaning floors — whatever odd job needed to be done. But when he was asked, "What do you do?" he would reply, "Bible translation." And he would be correct because every person on that team was working toward the larger goal, which was bigger than any one person of putting the Bible into the hands of the people around the world.

I think this is getting close to the attitude that Paul suggests, "Rejoice always, pray without ceasing, give thanks in all circumstances" (vv. 16-18). It's not about the money. It's not about the personal praise. What is it? It has to be that last part where Paul writes: "... for this is the will of God in Christ Jesus for you."

When my family went to Romania for a mission trip, my son, Nathan, joined me on the construction site. I went indoors to hang sheetrock and he stayed outdoors in the hot sun digging a ditch — one foot wide and three feet deep. The ground was awful. An adult had to break up the rocks and roots and Nathan had to get into the ditch and take out the pieces. It took forever.

The end of the first day, he said, "Dad, this is hard work. I don't like it." And I asked him if he knew what he was doing. He said, "Digging a ditch." "No," I said, "do you know what we are doing here? This building was once a communist office. We are converting it into four apartments that will house people temporarily who have been evicted from their apartments, lost their jobs, or are in crisis. That ditch you dug today will be filled with concrete. Concrete

21

blocks will be placed upon it. They will build a small room were they will install a wood burning water heater that will provide hot water for four families that don't have a home."

From that point on, whenever people asked Nathan what he was doing, he said, "Providing hot water for people living in emergency housing." Now, it was still ditch digging, it was still mixing concrete and pouring it. It was still stacking blocks. It was still hard work but now he could see his labor in terms of a providing a blessing.

That's the Fred Factor. It's about being a blessing. You can just deliver mail or you can have a relationship with the people on your route. You can dig a ditch or you can provide hot water. You can sell insurance or you can protect people in crisis. You can be in banking or you can support the economy and create more jobs. You can be a financial planner or you can help people send their children to college. See, it is the same job. And sometimes it isn't all that fun. So what is the difference? In the secular world, it is called the Fred Factor. Here, we call it being a blessing to others. "And whatever you do, in word or deed, do everything in the name of the Lord Jesus, giving thanks to God the Father through him" (Colossians 3:17). This means whatever you do, do it well as if you are serving Jesus himself. Or, let me put it another way. You don't have to be a doctor snatching people from the jaws of death. You don't have to be a lawyer defending the innocent and bringing to justice the guilty. You don't have to be a pastor preaching every Sunday to be a blessing. You can deliver the mail. You can dig ditches. You can provide the customer with a great product at a fair price. You can manage people with respect, integrity, and fairness. You can be a blessing by *rejoicing always, praying without ceasing, giving thanks in all circumstances.*

The reason I say that with confidence is because through faith Paul says that it is no longer you who live but Christ who lives within you (Galatians 2:20). Through faith, your life mirrors the image of the one who created you — let it shine. Through faith, you can do all things through Christ who strengthens you. That's why you can be a blessing because he was to you.

If you ask Jesus, "What do you do?" I doubt that he would pull out a pay stub. He probably would not answer that with a title on a business card or a degree on the wall. I doubt that he would even speak in terms of the global impact of being raised up at the fullness of time to atone for the collective sins of the world. No, I bet he would say, "I provide you with the way back to God. I provide you with the truth about this world. I provide you life — abundant, passionate life. And I provide you the opportunity to live — to live for others. You be my hands. You be my feet. You be my mouth. You be the blessing by letting your light so shine before others that they may see your good works and glorify your Father in heaven." Amen.

But Is It True?

*Now to God who is able to strengthen you according
to my gospel and the proclamation of Jesus Christ, according to the revelation of the mystery that was kept
secret for long ages but is now disclosed, and through
the prophetic writings is made known to all the Gentiles,
according to the command of the eternal God, to bring
about the obedience of faith.*

— Romans 16:25-26

Authors such as Lee Strobel, Nicky Gumbel, and Josh McDow-
ell have spoken around the world about these 300 prophecies of the
Old Testament and how they all point to Jesus. This cannot be mere
coincidence. It cannot be like playing the lottery. The evidence is
so overwhelming and the prophecies so compelling that one would
think that the only logical conclusion would be to say that it is true.

Unless you have the brain of a C. S. Lewis, faith doesn't come
through a logical, mathematical proof of Jesus as the Messiah. That
may certainly bolster your faith and add credence to your convic-
tions. But for most, we can be presented all the logical arguments
and still wonder late at night, alone in bed, "Is it true?"

Do you believe it? I'm not asking if you can prove it. I'm asking
if you believe it. You know, the virgin birth, the trip to Bethlehem,
no room in the inn, no crib for a bed, angels singing, shepherds
visiting. Do you think it really happened ... like that?

Apparently some who teach it don't think so. Professor Bart
Ehrman, head of the religious studies department at Chapel Hill,

has written a book with a clever title in the wave of *The Da Vinci Code*. It's called, *Misquoting Jesus: The Story Behind Who Changed the Bible and Why*. His premise is that we don't have any original, autographed copies of Matthew, Mark, Luke, or John. What we have are copies of copies. That much is true. But Professor Ehrman claims that since there is this gap between the original writing and the copies, the ancient scribes who copied these manuscripts shaped the Bible by sloppy mistakes or by their conscious changes to advance their own religious agenda. Thus, what we have in the Bible is, unfortunately, this very flawed, human-shaped collection of books that cannot be fully trusted.

So much for the mystery proclaimed by the prophets now revealed to us in Jesus.

Now, part of what Ehrman claims is absolutely true. It's true that before the printing press in the 1400s, scribes had to hand-copy the Bible word for word. It's true that there are discrepancies among the copies. It's true that changes were made. The most famous example is the story of the woman caught in adultery in John 8. The earliest manuscripts don't have it. It was probably added later by a scribe.

We don't have one manuscript saying that it was a virgin birth and the other saying that Jesus had a striking resemblance to Joseph. We don't have one manuscript saying that Jesus died on the cross and another saying he wiped off the blood and got back in the game. We don't have one manuscript that says Jesus rose from the dead and another saying, "No, he pretty much stayed dead." In other words, the discrepancies in the manuscripts are fairly minor and come down to an "and" or was it a "but." "Is" or was it "was." Was it an inn or a stable or a cave?

It seems that Ehrman wants to push these discrepancies a bit further by putting into question many of our cherished, biblical stories and widely held beliefs such as the Trinity, the divinity of Jesus, the miracles, and Jesus as the Messiah as nothing more than fairy tales coming from the alterations by ancient scribes. So, I come back to my original question: Do you believe it? Is it true? Did it happen the way the Bible recorded it? Do you believe that this story begins before the foundations of this world? Is this a story that is foretold by prophets centuries before it came to pass? Did this story burst forth, taking the world by surprise, at the fullness of time when God decided to smuggle himself into this world in the body of a poor, young peasant girl from Nazareth?

From the casual, outside observer, this story is filled with chaos and confusion. Plan? What plan? Everything is in disarray. A young girl engaged to one man gets pregnant and we know that the fiancé is not the father — betrayal. Convinced by angels and dreams that this is no ordinary pregnancy, the two stay together, enduring the heckling and ridicule of the townsfolk — scorn. As if that weren't enough, at precisely the time in which she was nine-and-a-half months pregnant and about to burst, they are ordered by a hostile, foreign government to travel the five days on a donkey from their hometown of Nazareth to a small, podunk village called Bethlehem — bad timing.

While they do make it to Bethlehem, as luck would have it, they arrive after a thousand other travelers who arrived earlier and reserved a room for their family, leaving this woman, obviously in labor, to find refuge in stable among the animals to give birth to her firstborn son — alone, young, scared, in a strange town, and having to deliver her baby all by herself. This whole night is "a series of unfortunate events."

And not just any baby. It would be one who exchanged a heavenly throne for a feeding trough, replaced flowing, eternal robes for a soiled diaper, left a heavenly castle for a barn, and gave up the company of angels for the company of peasants and shepherds. His hands, which once held stars in their places now were wrapped around a young, poor, unwed girl's finger.

Is it true that while chaos and confusion overwhelmed the day that God's plan was actually, deliberately, intentionally, and sovereignly unfolding? Is it true that God in the flesh would grow up to be a carpenter, be fine with being mistaken as a gardener, happy to have shepherds be his first visitors? Is it true that the King of kings would stoop down to wash feet, to touch the sick, to embrace the lonely? Is it true that the righteous one would stand to be ridiculed, mocked, and nailed to a crossbeam by sinful hands?

The ancient prophecy, the mystery of old unfolds this night. And somewhere between the presents, the out-of-town visitors, the candlelight, and the music you have to be asking, is it true? Or is it really, as some would suggest, just the imagination of a maverick, renegade scribe gone wild in the sixth century making the Christmas story as believable as the story of Jack and the beanstalk? You see, there comes a point in which that question is no longer reserved for academia or the subject of a book trying to ride on the successful coattails of *The Da Vinci Code* or casual conversation around eggnog. There comes a time in which that question, "Is it true?" becomes a matter of life and death.

The week before Christmas, I spend some time visiting older members of the congregation who cannot make it to church to bring them communion. I had one great visit with a woman who put that very question to me. After I had prepared the wine and bread, I opened up Luke 2 and read the Christmas story for her. As I read, she recited the story out loud with me from memory. We stumbled at some points. I was reading from a new translation. She recited from the original King James Version. When I said the shepherds were terrified and she recited, "And they were sore afraid."

She knew it by heart. She learned it as a child, taught it in Sunday school, and heard it annually for ninety years. But now, unable to get out of bed, she asked me when I was through, "Is it true? This story. Do you think it's true? I'm ninety years old now. I can't get out of bed. I think about death ... a lot. I wonder about heaven. I wonder if it is true ... because at ninety, I don't have much time left. Do you think it is true?"

I said, "I don't know if the streets are paved with gold. I don't know if the walls are filled with jewels. I don't know if it was a stable or a cave. I don't know if you will see angels with harps. But I do know this. We live in a fallen world in which darkness covers us like a blanket. Nowhere in scripture are we asked to naively deny the darkness. Nowhere in scripture do we receive a pep talk that convinces us that the darkness isn't really as bad as it seems. In fact, scripture tells us just the opposite. Scripture affirms that the darkness is called sin and that we are in bondage and that with Christmas, the light shines in the darkness and the darkness has not overcome it. What I do know is this — that this child born on Christmas came to restore that broken relationship with God by taking away the stain of sin and removing your guilt. I do know this — that because of Jesus, the dead will rise again. I do know this — that those who once walked in darkness are now children of the light. I do know this — because of Jesus, one day you will see the face of God and live."

She thought for a moment, nodded and said once again, "Oh, I know it's true. It's just that sometimes (and she paused, forced a brave smile), it's just that sometimes I am afraid."

I just held her hand and I asked, "Do you remember the first words out of the angel's mouth on that first Christmas when he announced the birth of Jesus?" She nodded. She knew it by heart. So I started — using the King James Version, "And the angel saith unto them ..." and she finished, "Fear not ... for I bring you good news of great joy." "Fear not," they said. "Be not afraid. And neither should you."

Because it is true. And not just because the Bible is trustworthy and the most complete of any ancient document with over 25,000 manuscripts, and not because the Bible is the most precise ancient document with less than 2% discrepancy among all those 25,000 manuscripts, and not because the Bible is the most historically accurate ancient document bar none with some manuscripts dating back to 125 AD.

That's pretty good and the evidence is overwhelming but that's not the only reason. Luther said that reason can only bring you so far, but for that final step, it takes a leap. That's why I believe, because this story is such a leap, such an extravagant gift. It's outrageous. No one would have dreamed up this stuff in the sixth century. I don't deserve a God who humiliated himself by becoming an illegitimate child, born in a barn, betrayed by a follower, denied by a friend, and beaten by the guilty. I don't deserve a God who would do something for me that I couldn't do for myself — die on the cross. I believe because I don't deserve that kind of extravagant gift. Do you?

Judas didn't ... but Jesus washed his feet.
Peter didn't ... but Jesus gave him the keys to heaven.
The shepherds didn't ... but they were the first to be invited.
Mary didn't ... but she was chosen.

29

The adulterer didn't ... but she was given a second chance.

The sinners and tax collectors didn't ... but Jesus welcomed them to his table.

And really, neither do we deserve it. Not on this night. It comes as an extravagant gift — and I'm taking that leap because I'm betting my life that this story is true. What are you betting your life on? If this were Texas Hold 'Em, I'd be all in. This is not some sophomoric, academic, mental exercise. It's not some topic for casual conversation or one more book idea for the shelves of Barnes and Noble. It is the only path, the only means, the only truth for us to remove the darkness of sin and despair and live in his marvelous light. Is it true? Do you believe it? This night? Not all the details; after all, scribes will be scribes and most of the details really don't matter except one — the detail of the promise. Do not be afraid for I bring you good news of great joy. For to you is born this day in the city of David, a Savior who is Christ the Lord. That's the one on this night worth betting your life on. Amen.

The Missing Piece

He it is who gave himself for us that he might redeem us from all iniquity and purify for himself a people of his own. — Titus 2:14

During this Christmas season, we usually get together with some other families and spend a couple of days together. Someone always brings out a jigsaw puzzle. We set up the card table and scatter the pieces. It's not like we spend all day huddled around the puzzle. We walk by, we eat, we grab a piece, connect it, eat, and finally, after much fanfare, celebration, and food, the puzzle is completed when that last piece is slipped into place. Then we eat. What a life!

Except those times when you come down to the very end and there's one piece missing. Isn't that awful? You never give yourself a high five for the 999 pieces already in place. No, it's that one last piece of the puzzle that has you so vexed.

Sometimes I look at this story of the birth of Jesus the same way — like some huge jigsaw puzzle. And, for the most part, all the pieces fit.

Like this piece. The baby — God becomes flesh. I get it. I know why God had to become a man. God wanted a relationship with us, to enter into our lives. But even more than that, for Jesus to take on the full penalty of our sin, suffer our punishment, endure our penalty, and die our death, he had to become fully human. I get it. It fits.

31

Or this piece. Bethlehem. Of course, Bethlehem. Micah said the Messiah will come from Bethlehem because that was the home of David and the Messiah had to come from David's family.

The piece about the census also fits. Mary and Joseph were living in Nazareth. They had no reason to go to Bethlehem except on orders of the emperor to be counted for more taxes. The census fits.

I know why Mary. Pure, faithful, obedient, favored. It fits.

I know why Joseph. Righteous, understanding, gracious. It fits.

Even the deep theological reason that Titus gives for the coming of Jesus — *to redeem us from all iniquity.* That piece is a corner piece to the whole puzzle. Of course it fits.

Even the ordinary piece. A peasant family from a no-name village. Nothing special. Simple folk. Uneducated. It fits. Even the name of Jesus piece. It fits. In the first century it was an ordinary name. There must have been ten Jesuses at his village. If he were born today, it would have been like Joe or Sam or John. Why? Because it fits. King Herod sent troops out to kill this new king of the Jews but he was looking for a majestic, full grown, military start up looking to conquer Herod's kingdom and set up his own government. He wasn't looking for the ordinary Jesus.

You see, it fits. It all fits. Since the foundation of the earth, God had every piece to this puzzle perfectly fit to bring forth his Son at the fullness of time. Nine hundred and ninety-nine pieces are in place. It should be time to celebrate. Except there's a hole, isn't there? A missing piece. Luke says, "there was no room for them in the inn."

If the details of the Bible matter, if the Bible is something more than just creative writing, why include this detail, this piece? Does it fit?

Oh, I know why there was no room — Bethlehem was over-run by other peasants who were in town for the same census. The rooms were all taken. But if the Lord God almighty, the king of the universe, can open up a parking space for me right in front of the mall on December 23, couldn't he find one space for Jesus?

We can't believe for a moment that this was an oversight by God or that God somehow forgot to make the reservation. This event had been planned down to the smallest piece for centuries. No, this piece has to fit, they all fit, but how? No room in the inn. Is it just because a stable is a logical place for shepherds to visit? Is it just because a stable is so ordinary? Is it just because the very thought of Jesus without a room is so pitiful and makes for a great nativity scene?

There was no room for them in the inn. Why? I used to think that it fit the whole humility theme. You know, shepherds, peasants, young unwed mother, no crib for a bed. The gospel always turns our world upside down. It always comes as a surprise. The last will be first, the first will be last. To be great, you must be a servant. To live, you must die. What greater twist, what greater turn to the gospel to have the King of kings and Lord of lords born in a barn?

But when I tried to fill that hole with this piece, the lines didn't quite line up. The colors didn't quite blend. It was close. But not quite.

Sometimes when you are working on a jigsaw puzzle, you need to step back, get a different perspective, turn the piece ever so slightly and then try it again.

No room in the inn. Can you imagine that night? It's eighty miles from Nazareth to Bethlehem. She's tired. She's pregnant. Not much to eat. It's late when they arrive and Murphy's Law goes into effect — it's late, it's cold, they have no room, no family, neither one knows "nothin' about birthin' no babies," and now she goes into labor — I bet it was raining, too. No room. Not for you. Not here. You, Jesus — go away! Go anywhere but here.

It starts there. A life of rejection. It doesn't start with Jesus' cry from the cross — "My God, my God, why have you forsaken me?" It doesn't begin with Peter — "I do not know the man." It doesn't begin with Judas — thirty pieces of silver. It doesn't begin with Jewish leaders plotting to kill him. The rejection begins here, in Bethlehem, the very first day he enters our world, by an innkeeper who had no room for Jesus. It begins there and continues today here, in the hearts of those who still have no room for Jesus. Not here. Not you. Go away. You are not welcome. Not in my life.

Rejection. Rejected by the very ones he came to save. Rejected by a world that loves the darkness. Rejected by those who have no room, no time, no need for a Savior. Does that fit? Unfortunately, it fits.

No room. No room. Not in the inn. Not anywhere. Did Jesus ever have a room? Was he ever welcomed? I suppose he had a room in Nazareth where he grew up — though the Bible says nothing about these early years. When he is twelve and his parents lost him in Jerusalem for a couple of days, remember where they found him? The temple. Remember what Jesus said to his frantic parents? "Did you not know that I must be in my Father's house?" (Luke 2:4a). Bet he had a room there.

Strange. As far as we know, as an adult, Jesus was homeless. We can go to Mount Vernon to see the home of George Washington. But Jesus has no home. In fact, when one disciple said that he would follow Jesus anywhere, Jesus said, "Foxes have dens to live in, and the birds have nests, but the Son of Man has no place even to lay his head" (Matthew 8:20).

From the moment he was born, we gave him our very worst — from a stable to a cross. We gave him our very worst. And yet he exposed himself to the full dangers of this world, from a drafty, dirty stable to a cross for one reason — not to find himself a home. He didn't need one. Instead, he came to give you a home. He chose the least so you could have the most. He chose the cross so you could have a place at the table. He chose to die so that you would never be left out in the cold. That's the missing piece.

We reject him for so many reasons — no room in the inn, no room in my heart, no room in my calendar, no room in my priorities. It is a rejection that leads right to the cross — you, Jesus, must die! And yet it is Jesus who rejects our rejection and says with amazing grace, "In my Father's house there are many rooms; if it were not so, would I have told you I go to prepare a place for you? And when I go and prepare a place for you, I will come again and will take you to myself, so that where I am you may be also" (John 14:2-3).

See, that's the missing piece, the way God had pictured it. The Bible says that you were made not for this world but you were made for eternity. This is not your home any more than a stable is a home for Jesus. The Bible calls your earthly body a tent, which will one day be torn down and replaced with a home that God has made for you.

That fits. The picture is complete. Now, what about your picture? Any holes? The picture you had of the perfect family, the perfect job, the perfect life, the perfect Christmas? What about your picture? Is it complete? Or is there still one piece missing? It's strange, isn't it? Like this jigsaw puzzle, you can have 999 pieces in place. For the most part, it looks pretty good — can't complain, much. But it is the hole that reminds us that the picture is not perfect, it's not complete, it's not right. There is that hole. Feel it?

Study after study, poll after poll tells us over and over again that we are busier than ever, getting more done than ever, making more money than ever, and yet we are more unhappy today than ever before. Why? It's not the 999 pieces in place. It's that one hole. A hole that we try to fill with more activities, more money, more pleasure — but it can only be filled by this same piece we have here tonight, by this one the world has rejected but who has not rejected you.

"He it is who gave himself for us that he might redeem us from all iniquity and purify for himself a people of his own" (Titus 2:14).

That's the missing piece. Jesus, the rejected one, who comes to you this night saying, "I know you have no room for me in the inn. You have no room for me in your heart. You have no room for me in your schedule. You have no room for me in your family, your work, your future. The only place you made room for me was a cross. But it was for that reason I came according to the perfect plan of God, to fill that hole in your picture, to erase that guilt from your sin, to remove that fear of your death with a promise — I go to prepare a home for you. So that where I am — there you will be also, one day, together with me in my Father's house."

That's the missing piece in the picture — your picture. Isn't it? Amen.

The Fullness Of Time

But when the fullness of time had come, God sent his
Son, born of a woman, born under the law, in order to
redeem those who were under the law, so that we might
receive adoption as children. — Galatians 4:4-5

Throughout the New Testament, there are numerous verses that say something about fulfillment. Jesus said, "These are my words which I spoke to you while I was still with you, that all things which are written about me in the law of Moses and the prophets and the psalms must be fulfilled" (Luke 24:44). On the cross, Jesus said, "I am thirsty" (John 19:28). He said this in order to fulfill the scriptures. Paul wrote, "But when the fullness of time had come, God sent his Son, born of a woman, born under the law ..." (Galatians 4:4). The fullness of time. What does that mean?

There are roughly 300 prophetic references written over a 1,000-year period about the Messiah in the Old Testament that narrow the field down to the true identity of the Messiah. First, there is the bloodline. From Abraham to Isaac to Jacob to Judah to David, the bloodline has a strong and definite line. However, by judging the overpopulation of Bethlehem during the census, those in the line of David are very numerous.

Second, there are the prophecies. Of those who are descendants of David, the prophecies concerning him narrow the field even more. We know that the Messiah would be born in Bethlehem (Malachi 5:2), betrayed by a friend with whom he breaks bread (Psalm 41:9), for thirty pieces of silver (Zechariah 11:12), abandoned by his disciples (Zechariah 13:7), die a death similar to crucifixion including pierced hands and feet pierced (Psalm 22), his clothes will be gambled away (Psalm 22:18), not a bone was broken (Psalm 34:20), though his side will be pierced (Zechariah 12:10), he will die among thieves and sinners (Isaiah 53:12), pray for his persecutors (Isaiah 53:12), buried in a rich man's tomb (Isaiah 53:9), whose death took on all the sins of the world (Isaiah 53).

Many authors have outlined in more detail how all 300 prophecies of Jesus point to only one man. The sheer statistical possibilities that land directly on Jesus are staggering. But I want to look at the phrase Paul uses that Jesus came "at the fullness of time." Paul isn't referring to the fulfillment of the prophecies but how God brought forth Jesus at just the right time in history.

At the fullness of time. What does that mean? It means what Jeremiah 33:14 promises that "The day will come, says the Lord, when I will do for Israel and Judah all the good I have promised them. At that time I will bring to the throne of David a righteous descendant and he will do what is just and right throughout the land." What does that mean? It means what John proclaims in 1:14 "So the Word became flesh and dwelt among us, full of grace and truth. And we have seen his glory, the glory of the only Son of the Father." What does that mean? That means our God was not passively waiting for a break in the action to bring forth his Son, but God actively set forth his hand in world history to bring about the coming of his Son in a window of time in all of recorded history of about fifty years. Let me explain.

For these prophecies to come true, it was going to happen in the Middle East. In other words, we probably don't have to study Chinese or ancient Australian Aborigines to find the Messiah. This was going to take place in the Middle East. The question was, *"When?"*

I don't have to tell you that this area of the world has had more wars, more blood spilled than perhaps anywhere else on earth. But there was a short, fifty-year window, in which the Messiah could appear.

The stage was set in 587 when the Babylonians captured Jerusalem and sent Daniel, Shadrach, Meshach, and Abednego into captivity in what is now Iraq. For forty years, the Jews were held in captivity until Cyrus of Persia freed them forty years later. Many of the Jews returned to Israel under the leadership of Nehemiah to rebuild the walls. However, most scattered throughout all of Asia Minor. This will be important 500 years later.

The Greeks conquered this area in 333 BC. What they brought was a unity of language and a hunger for philosophy. By the time of Jesus, everyone was speaking primarily Greek. Hebrew was a dead language. Communication wasn't a problem. And there was a hunger for new teachings, new learning, new philosophies. Keep those two things in mind.

Around 60 BC, Rome conquered this area and several things happened. First, the peace of Rome extended from the middle of Europe, down the Italian Peninsula through Turkey and Greece and into the Middle East. This included some 55 million inhabitants. With no danger of war, roads were established for safe and quick travel — all roads literally lead to Rome. There was homogeneity throughout the Roman empire that the language and culture from the east could be heard, understood, and experienced all the way to the west. As for religion, the emperor demanded that everyone in the Roman empire worship the emperor. The only exception was granted to the Jews. They were stubborn, they were resilient and they were on the fringe of the empire and not seen as a major threat.

While Rome experienced peace and prosperity, Judaism was in crisis. In the first century BC, four distinct sects of Judaism emerged: the Pharisees, Sadducees, Essenes, and the Zealots. To the Jew, there were major distinctions between these four. To the Romans, they were all lumped together as Judaism, an exception to emperor worship. These four sects continued until between 70 AD when Rome sacked Jerusalem and 90 AD at the Council of Jamnia.

When Christianity arose with the death and resurrection of Jesus, Christians worshiped side by side with the Jews for about fifty years. The Jews saw them as a fifth sect within Judaism but Rome did not see Christianity as a separate religion. It was almost as if Christianity lay hidden in the womb of Judaism until it was birthed. For in 90, the Jews kicked the Christians out of the synagogues and Rome recognized them as a separate religion. However, by then, Christianity could not be contained. Because of the unity of language, the hunger for new teaching, the peace of Rome, the road system, the homogeneity — Christianity spread like wildfire. Why did it spread so quickly? Remember who Paul first went to in his missionary journeys? To the Jews and synagogues. Why were there so many Jews and synagogues throughout all of Asia Minor? Go back 500 years ago when Cyrus of Persia freed the Jews from Babylon. Instead of returning to Israel, they scattered throughout this region, creating strategic outposts and dry kindling so that when Christianity ignited, it spread like wildfire throughout the Roman empire. Forty years after it began in a land in which there was no mass communication, Christianity became a dominant force in the Roman empire to warrant an all-out persecution by the state.

That's the fullness of time to which Paul refers. It is a short, fifty-year window in all of history that the Messiah could have been born. God not only fulfilled all the prophecies from the Old Testament in Jesus but from the foundation of the world, set the historical events in motion so that at the fullness of time his Son would be born.

No other person in all of history has affected the world to the extent of Jesus Christ. No matter who you say he is, no other religion, person, philosophy, empire, or anything else has had this impact. And to think his ministry lasted only three years. He never wrote a book, had no formal education, traveled less than 300 miles, and held no public office. He died penniless, humiliated, and alone. We know very little about his life. What we know most is the day of his death. And yet today, about two billion people call him Lord.

Do you see? This world is not spinning out of control or ruled by chaos. Ours is not a distant God who passively sits back waiting to be found. Ours is a God deeply committed to our eternal life and willingly manipulated world events, set in motion each piece of the puzzle, and announced his promise to you that in the fullness of time, God sent his Son, born of a woman, subject to the law to buy freedom for us who were slaves to the law, so that he could adopt us as his very own children. Amen.

It's God's Will?

... he chose us in Christ before the foundation of the world to be holy and blameless before him in love. He destined us for adoption as his children through Jesus Christ, according to the good pleasure of his will.
— Ephesians 1:4-5

Harold is 81 years old and one day after worship he came up to me and said, "There is something I want you to preach on before too long. When I was eleven years old, my mother died. The good people at the church kept on telling me it was God's will for her to die. Do you think that it was God's will to take the life of a young boy's mom? Now that I'm getting older, I plan on seeing her again, soon. Before I do, I'd like to hear what you think about God's will."

That question and Paul's words in Ephesians 1 raise all sorts of questions. I bet before his mother died, the doctors worked hard on her for some time, using their very best medical knowledge. Were they working against God's will? I don't know the circumstances surrounding her death, but if it was a car accident — was God at the wheel? If it was cancer — did God send those renegade cells? If it was self-inflicted — did God lead her down that darkened pit of depression and hopelessness?

Do you see the dilemma? On the one side I can only assume those church folks were offering words of comfort to young Harold, "It's God's will." They wanted him to know that God is in control. This world is not governed by dumb luck, the stars, or chaos, but by a sovereign Lord who is overseeing every detail of our lives. Not

41

a sparrow falls to the ground without his knowledge. Every hair on your head is counted. The psalm says that you were knit together in your mother's womb. Before a word is on your lips, God knows it. Every day of your life is recorded in his book, laid out before a single day ever passed. He chose you from the foundations of the earth. It's all God's will.

And for the most part those words of comfort work — until when? Until the mother of an eleven-year-old boy dies. Until that child runs out into the street. Until airplanes are flown into twin towers. And then ... and then we are left with even more questions. Questions about the goodness of God, questions about the power of God, questions about the existence of God. Is it God's will?

This is not merely the question of an eleven-year-old boy but during the Reformation, this was the key issue at stake. Do we have free will or is everything predestined? You come to terms with this, and you will understand the central teaching of the Bible, the reason for the Reformation, and the foundation by which this church stands or falls — justification by faith through grace. You miss this, and you will forever be stuck in a quagmire of unanswerable questions and dead ends.

Let's begin with a definition. Predestination. You hear two parts. "Pre" which means "beforehand" — as in a pregame warm up before the game or prehistoric, which means before there was any formal, written history.

The second part is "destination." It refers to where you are headed. When I go to the airport, they ask me, "What is your final destination?" I always say, "Heaven." And when the ticket agent doesn't think that's very clever, I softly say, "Minneapolis." But that's the meaning of the word, right? Destination: Where are you ultimately headed?

Now, put them together. Predestination means knowing beforehand where you are going to end up — before you even get there. It's not a word or idea I made up — nor did Luther or Calvin. It comes right out of the writings of Paul.

*Long ago, even before he made the world, God loved us
and chose us in Christ to be holy and without fault in his*

42

*eyes. His unchanging plan has always been to adopt us
into his own family ... God's secret plan has now been
revealed to us ... for he chose us from the beginning,
and all things happen just as he decided long ago.*
                              — Ephesians 1:4-5, 9, 11 (NIV)

*For those whom he foreknew he also predestined to
be conformed to the image of his Son, in order that he
might be the first-born among many brethren. And those
whom he predestined he also called; and those whom
he called he also justified; and those whom he justified
he also glorified.*   — Romans 8:29-30

Predestination. Knowing beforehand where you are going to end up — before you even get there. But does this mean that God foresees the future or does it mean that he forecauses the future. See the difference? Foreseeing is God simply knowing the future. Forecausing is God dictating the details of life in order to cause the future. This is what Luther called the *core* teaching and it comes down to one question, "Do we have free will or does everything happen according to God's will?"

Let's see how different branches have answered that question.

The Roman Catholic church would say, "A little." They teach that we are fallen, sinful creatures — but not totally. If we participate, even in the slightest bit, through good works, confession, giving, service, worship through free will — then God will reward with grace. God foresees the future but he isn't causing the future. That's up to people working in conjunction with God.

John Calvin, father of the Presbyterian church, said, "There is no free will." We are fallen, sinful creatures who cannot respond to God. God numbers our days, there are no accidents, everything happens according to God's purpose. God chooses some people to go to heaven and some people to go to hell through his divine election. God doesn't just know the future, he causes the future — thus we have no free will.

And then a Dutch Pastor named Jacob Arminius, a student of Calvin, preached this to his congregation. They thought, "Without free will, the cards are already dealt, the final chapter is already written. I might as well eat, drink, and be merry because God has already chosen me for heaven or hell. I'm a drunk because I'm destined to be a drunk. I'm an adulterer because I'm destined to be an adulterer." Such fatalism didn't make sense to Arminius so he taught we have free will to accept, decide, and choose Jesus Christ as our Savior. From this group we have the Baptists, Assembly of God, and Pentecostals.

Luther said that when it comes to our day-to-day living — getting a job, finding a spouse, studying for a test, there is complete free will. You are a liar because you chose to lie. You are an adulterer because you chose to cheat. On this horizontal level, this day-to-day living, God is not causing the details. Oh, he foresees them; he knows the choices you will make. But he doesn't cause them. There is free will in how you choose to live.

But in our relationship with God, in our final destination, in matters of heaven and hell, Luther taught that there is no free will. Luther called it a bound will because deep within this heart lives a rebel who is spitting apple into the face of God. Deep within this heart lives a rebel who wants to be free from the confines of God. Deep within this heart lives a rebel who, when asked to make a choice or a decision about Jesus, this rebel made it loud and clear, "Kill him, crucify him."

Sin is not simply lying, cheating, and stealing that we could overcome if we just tried harder. Sin is a condition, a state of fallenness. I am in bondage to sin and cannot free myself. The good I want to do, I don't do. The bad things I don't want to do, that's what I end up doing. This will is rebellious by nature, it is bound by sin. Luther taught the third article of the creed by saying, "I cannot by my own understanding or effort believe in Jesus Christ as my Lord or come to him." It is the work of the Holy Spirit.

The only hope I have is Jesus who rescues me from death by paying the price for sin and choosing us, as Paul writes in Ephesians 1. This does not mean that God directs and causes every detail of our lives. Much of what happens grieves the very heart of God. But predestination is about where we are headed. Where will we spend eternity? More importantly, how will you get there? Will your salvation come from your own rebellious hands spitting apple into the face of God, chanting with the crowds, "crucify him," or from a grace-filled God who, as Paul said, "chose us from the beginning, before the world began, and called us as his own." Do you see why Luther said this is the key issue of the Reformation? You grasp this and suddenly justification through faith by God's grace makes sense.

I know it's confusing. In fact, while Luther thought this was the core teaching, he didn't talk about it much because people misunderstood it. They ask dead-end questions, fall into fatalism, and say dumb things to an eleven-year-old at his mother's funeral. For Luther, predestination was always meant to be a source of comfort not fatalism. God knit you together in your mother's womb. He knows your lying down and your getting up. He goes to prepare a place for you and when that time is right, he will come back personally and take you to himself. You see? Sovereign grace.

In chapter 2 of Rick Warren's book, *The Purpose-Driven Life*, he says that nothing is an accident, nothing happens outside of God's plan. All the details of your life have been scripted from the foundations of the earth. God has a plan, a purpose for your life.[1] This is straight, God-caused predestination to the extreme. God not only foreknows what will happen but God is causing it to happen. Trouble is, later on in the book, Warren switches gears and talks about the need for each one of us to make a decision to believe in Jesus. You stand at a fork in the road. It could go either way. Choose to follow him. Start obeying him today. It's all up to you. And you have to ask, what happened to the sovereign plan of God where there are no accidents? Warren writes out of the Arminian branch of the Reformation.

In many ways, Warren's book is great. But here, Luther teaches just the opposite. Not every detail of our daily lives is dictated by God or a part of his divine plan. We live in a fallen world in which planes are flown into towers, wars rage on for years, children are struck by cars, and, yes, Harold, sometimes eleven-year-old boys have to grow up without a mom. I hate that. And I can only imagine that God does, too. But he promises us his presence, his strength, his comfort to make it through. He also promises more than that. He promises that there will come a day, and you have his word on this, there will come a day when he will make all things new. He will wipe away every tear from your eye, erase every doubt from your mind, turn darkness into light, and he will once and for all, destroy death — that final enemy. "And those whom he predestined he also calls; and those whom he called he also justifies; and those whom he justifies he also glorifies" (Romans 8:30). Do not be afraid, Harold, for ours is a sure and certain hope. Only believe because we know how the story ends. The kingdom is ours forever. Amen.

---

1. Rick Warren, *The Purpose-Driven Life* (Grand Rapids, Michigan: Zondervan, 2002).

The Epiphany Of Our Lord
Ephesians 3:1-12

Epiphany: All About You!

... God has given me this special ministry of announcing his favor to you Gentiles. — Ephesians 3:2 (NLT)

Is it just my imagination or have we really become more self-absorbed over the past decades? Look at the progression for magazines. In the 1950s, we had *Life* magazine, which pretty much covered everything around us. In the 1960s, we narrowed that scope down to *People*. We weren't too concerned about other forms of life, just our own. In the 1970s we had *US Magazine*. Not them. It's all about *us*. In the 1980s, we specialized. We wanted our uniqueness featured so we started buying *Teen* magazine, *Active Living*, and women's and men's magazines. In the 1990s, we grew tired of those in our group. We wanted something more fascinating and exciting so we began reading *Self* magazine — what a great name! And beginning with the 2006 *Time* magazine, we have narrowed that scope even further — *me*. It's all about me. I'm the one who ought to be celebrated, affirmed, and awarded. Do you know what I'm talking about? I'm referring to 2006 *Time* magazine's "Person of the Year" — *you*! You are the person of the year. Each year, *Time* magazine selects a person of the year who has made the greatest impact during the previous year. And that person was *you*! Did you see it coming? Did you guess it? Of course not, though secretly you knew you always deserved it. Congratulations!

So when *Time* selected you as the person of the year, from their perspective, you should feel very flattered. You beat out all the competition. *Time* wrote this:

47

... who actually sits down after a long day at work and says, "I'm not going to watch Lost *tonight. I'm going to turn on my computer and make a movie starring my pet iguana? I'm going to mash up 50 Cent's vocals with Queen's instrumentals? I'm going to blog about my state of mind or the state of the nation or the* steak-frites *at the new bistro down the street?" Who has the time and that energy and that passion?*

The answer is, you *do. And for seizing the reins of the global media, for founding and framing the new digital democracy, for working for nothing and beating the pros at their own game,* Time*'s Person of the Year for 2006 is* you.[1]

In retrospect, we should have guessed it. After all, we live in a world that's all about you — your desires, your wants, your needs. I no longer have to buy a CD for the one or two songs that I like. I can create my own playlist on my own iPod. I no longer have to put up with one movie that CBS plays on Sunday night — commercials and all. Blockbuster has a million titles — and now they will mail my picks to me or I can have a movie on demand or download it to my own player. I no longer have to mess with malls, people, clerks, post offices, grocery stores — I can shop online. Because after all, I am the person of the year.

From MySpace to Blogs to YouTube, it's all about me. Really, when did we get to the point of this overinflated ego to think that my face, my thoughts, my videos, my pictures are so interesting, so unique, that you should really check out my website? When did we get to the point that we feel so indisposable that we can interrupt a lunch with a friend to talk to someone else on the phone — and say nothing at all? I've got a pastor friend who does campus ministry and has told me that in the past ten years he has seen a dramatic change on campus. Ten years ago, he could walk the campus, make eye contact, say, "Hi," or chat with a student. Today, no one is talking. They are not even making eye contact. They are listening, watching, or talking — alone and plugged in, alone with these "weapons of mass distraction."

Now, despite my ranting and raving, to be sure our high-tech age has enabled more people to stay in touch with family and friends around the world. I understand that. And we have become empowered to express ourselves and discover information on our own using the web. All good things. From email to blogsites to posting pictures, we are more connected than ever before. I'm just convinced we have fewer relationships then ever before. I'm just convinced our heart no longer aches for the other. This hour of worship just might be the closest you will be to a living, breathing person all week because there's no time or desire to look into the eyes of another because it has really turned out to be all about me. *Time* magazine confirmed it. I am the person of the year.

In the early 1500s, Nicholas Copernicus was a Polish astronomer who put forth a radical theory that rocked both the scientific and theological worlds. He said that the sun and not the earth was the center of the universe. The earth was just one of many small planets circling a larger heavenly body. Everyone gasped. The implications were enormous. Suddenly, we were not the center of the universe. Suddenly, the sun and moon didn't rise and fall on me. Suddenly I was so very insignificant.

The church fought him on theological reasons. "We are the pinnacle of creation, designed in the image of God. How dare you," the priests said. Science fought him on empirical reasons. "We are the top of the food chain and called to have dominion." But Copernicus held his ground and literally put us in our place, causing not only a stir but a revolution.

In his book, *It's Not About Me*, Max Lucado coins a phrase that might be helpful in light of *Time*'s Person of the Year. He says that we need a "Copernican shift" of the heart.[2] It's not about me. It's about the one who created me. It is for his purpose and his glory that we have our life and breath and being. Luther called for us to die daily in our baptism and to remember that it is not about me but about Christ who dwells in me through faith. And if it were left to Luther, he said, he would bring it all to ruin. Paul put it this way, "Whatever you do in word or deed, do everything in the name of the Lord Jesus, giving thanks to God the Father through him" (Colossians 3:17).

Epiphany shows us how to get over ourselves and have this Copernicus revolution of the heart. We follow the journey of the magi across the desert. It is a journey that slows us down long enough to put away the cell phones and turn off the computer to see that I didn't put the stars in their courses, I didn't dictate the rise of the tides, I didn't maneuver the earth around the sun, and I certainly didn't strap on a cross for someone else.

It is in the quiet journey of Epiphany that Paul's words suddenly come to us as a surprise. There is a plan, a secret plan laid out from the foundations of the earth that has not been carried out through Jesus. A plan that reveals God's special favor and mighty powers for you.

That's when the message of Epiphany finally takes us by surprise. That the one who put the stars in their places and commands the tides to rise and fall would be born in a barn, reduced to a baby, suffer insults, beatings, and a cross until he descended into the very pit of hell. Why would he do such a thing?

Because it really is all about you. He did it just for you. In Jesus' heart — let's be real — you are not the person of the year. You are the person for all eternity. That's why he did it all. Because of his favor to you. It's his plan for you from the foundations of the earth come true in Jesus. It's is all about you. Sometimes it takes a long journey, a quiet night, and a star to remind you just how important you are to God. Amen.

---

1. Lev Grossman, "Time's Person of the Year: You," *Time* magazine, December 25, 2006.

2. Max Lucado, *It's Not About Me* (Nashville, Tennessee: Thomas Nelson, Inc., 2004), p. 5.

The Baptism Of Our Lord
Epiphany 1
Ordinary Time 1
Acts 19:1-7

A Grandmother's Touch

Then what baptism did you experience?
— Acts 19:3a (NLT)

It's texts like this one from Acts 19 that create so many mis-understandings and downright disagreements about baptism for all ages.

There was a story about a mom who glanced out through her kitchen window at her children playing across the yard. It was one of those games children play that looks complicated to the outside eye but for them it makes perfect sense. They had brought out a shovel and dug a hole in the soft dirt of the garden, dragged over the garden hose, and had an array of dolls lying on the ground. Then the process began. The daughter picked up the dolls one at a time, soaked them with water, handed it to her brother who threw it into the hole. Unable to figure out this game, the mom went out and asked what they were doing. The boy said, "We are playing baptism. Watch." Her sister picked up a doll, drenched it with water and said, "In the name of the Father and the Son," and then, handing the doll to her brother, she concluded the line, "and into-the-hole-it-goes."

Baptism. It is one of the immovable cornerstones of our faith ... and yet, there is a lot of misunderstanding about it. And if it isn't out and out misunderstanding, there is much disagreement about what it is and what it does between different denominations. Part of the reason is because scripture doesn't outline a consistent example of baptism. Jesus and many others were baptized as adults and yet in the book of Acts it says that entire households were baptized. Does that include children?

51

In some cases, the Holy Spirit comes first (as in Pentecost) and at other times it comes after baptism (as in our story from Acts 19). Then there seems to be John's baptism which is different from Jesus' baptism. If there is such confusion within scripture, there surely must be confusion within our churches today.

Let me address some of those concerns with a story. In my first church in Florida, I met a young family in the park near our home where many children played together. Cathy and John were new to town, had a child my daughter's age, and were looking for a church. I had one I could recommend wholeheartedly. They started coming and got connected quickly.

Before they joined, however, they asked me over to their apartment. They had a question about which they needed some counsel. The wife, Cathy, in her late twenties, was not raised in a church home. Her parents had left the church in the late '60s never to return. Church was new to her. Her interest in Christianity, however, was piqued during college through some conversations and Bible study on campus. The more she studied, the more she believed ... and the angrier she got. She was angry at her parents. The only person she could talk to about this was her grandma, the spiritual matriarch of the family — a devout Catholic woman who lived her faith on a daily basis. She was safe. She understood. She listened to Cathy who talked about this new faith in Jesus and the regret, even anger, at her parents for not providing the basic, spiritual foundation in her life. Cathy felt robbed, particularly during her early years, of the joy that she felt now. "Why (and this is where her blood began to boil) why, they didn't even have me baptized!"

With that the grandmother winked, smiled, and said, "Oh, you're baptized, all right. Over there. In the sink. By me. When you were two months old." Evidently, Grandma got some tips from her priest. She decided 24 years ago that no grandchild of hers was going to be denied the gift of baptism.

"So," Cathy asked me, "am I baptized?"

Let's begin there with the first question: "Is Cathy baptized?" The answer is, "Yes." What makes baptism work is not the location. Baptisms can be done outside of the church building. What makes baptism work is not some special water blessed by a bishop or from the Jordan River. What makes baptism work is not the person doing the baptism — grandmother or priest. Certainly, whenever possible an ordained pastor ought to perform baptisms but not because he or she has special powers. The pastor should only for the sake of good order — that there is some continuity and intentionality from baptism to baptism. In an emergency, however, a nurse or parent or grandparent can baptize a child.

The second question is: "Does Cathy have to be rebaptized in order to join the church?" The answer is, "No." We believe in *one* baptism for the forgiveness of sins. To be rebaptized casts a shadow of a doubt upon the promise and goodness of God that he could not possibly do it the first time and now needs help with Cathy's consent to make the promise work. To be sure, many people who submit to rebaptism don't do it out of doubt. They do it as a visible means by which they reaffirm their faith and commitment in Jesus. But there are other ways to recommit, reaffirm, and renew your baptism than to do it all over again as if God were unable to do it right the first time.

The third question is more difficult: "What if Cathy had never come to faith? Would her baptism one day guarantee her a place at the heavenly banquet?" Not as easy, is it? Not as easy as simply "Yes" or "No" like the other two. I need to say a couple of things, first. Number one, baptism is not just fire insurance to protect yourself from the eternal pit. Baptism is about enjoying the benefits of God's grace right now in this world. If baptism is reduced to some mindless, meaningless, ritual that is done simply because your grandma thinks it's a good idea or to somehow safeguard you from hell no matter the life you lead or the lack of faith, then I suppose the answer is, "No." There is nothing in scripture and nothing from the Reformation that would suggest that we are justified by baptism alone. We are saved by grace through faith ... and not just any faith — faith in Jesus Christ.

To be sure, the primary actor in baptism is God. God forgives. God names. God claims. God welcomes. It is true that the parents make a promise to raise this child in the knowledge of their baptism but the fact that we most often perform baptism on infants highlights that baptism is an act of sheer grace.

But we live in that grace. Parents make promises to raise children in that grace. We have Sunday school classes that teach this grace. When baptism becomes some mindless, meaningless ritual that is used as some magical protection against hell regardless of faith, regardless of being in community, regardless of life — well, you miss the point. Baptism wasn't meant to be that. However, we cannot answer that question, "Yes" or "No," because that is not our decision. Such a question steps over the boundary between our jurisdiction and God's jurisdiction. It's speculation. God alone decides who sits at his heavenly banquet. God alone judges over a person's ultimate destination. God alone. Our jurisdiction is to plant the seed and water the soil by teaching, preaching ... and, yes, baptizing in the name of the Father, Son, and Holy Spirit.

The final question: "When did God enter Cathy's life?" Let me ask that a different way: "Was God present in Cathy's life before she felt his presence, before she believed in Jesus, before she came to faith?" *Absolutely.* The psalmist writes, "You formed my inward parts, you knit me together in my mother's womb. Wonderful are your works. You know me" (Psalm 139:13-14).

As Jesus was being kicked and dragged to the top of that hill to be pierced with nails, remember his words? "Father, forgive them ... they don't know what they are doing." Before they confessed their sins, before they turned to God, before one Roman soldier accepted Jesus Christ as Lord, God was already there — bathing them with his grace, showering them with his forgiveness, engulfing them with his presence.

God was there. God was in Cathy's life long before she realized it. Pushing, poking, prodding, and guiding her toward faith. Cathy didn't so much accept God as God accepted her. Cathy didn't so much decide for Jesus as Jesus decided for her. Cathy didn't so much find God as God found her and knit her together in her mother's womb. God has always been a part of Cathy's life even before she knew it.

There will come times when you feel so strong in your faith and certain of God's presence that you will feel as if you can move mountains. But there will be those valleys, too, in which God seems

54

so very distant. Doubt will eat away at your faith like a cancer. Questions that chip away at your beliefs will plague your heart. If you have never gone through those times of doubt and felt the absence of God's presence, you either are lying or you don't have a pulse. We all go through what is called the dark night of the soul.

It is then, perhaps more than any other time, the gift and the promise of baptism make the most sense. They are not gifts that turn on or turn off like a switch depending on whether or not I feel it. God is not present only when my faith is strong enough on a particular day to experience him. Even when my faith goes through a lifelong roller coaster, the promise of God remains constant. With a splash of water and the proclamation of the word, the promise is there ... to remind you that your sins are forgiven, even before you are ready to confess; to reassure you that you belong, even before you have turned to come back home; and to claim you as one of his very own, even if that promise was made in the kitchen sink at the hands of a faithful grandmother. Amen.

Faith vs. Good Works

"All things are lawful for me," but not all things are beneficial. "All things are lawful for me," but I will not be dominated by anything. — 1 Corinthians 6:12

In 1 Corinthians 6, Paul touches on a topic that has captivated Christians and fragmented churches for centuries. What is the relationship between our faith and good works? If I am saved by faith alone, then what are my limits?

There is a certain order, a certain logic, a certain progression to life that just makes sense. If I work hard, then I will get a raise. If I study hard, then I will get a good grade. If I eat my vegetables, then I get my dessert. There is no free lunch. Right? There is this ladder mentality we all have, a progression that makes sense. Step by step, we must work our way to the top of the ladder.

When the early church fathers were trying to figure out how a person gets to heaven, they turned to this ladder theology. Pelagius taught that if you want to get to heaven, you had better start climbing. No one will do it for you. It all depends on your choice and free will to start climbing. Go to church. Say your prayers. Feed the hungry. Contribute money. Step by step you will eventually earn your place in heaven.

It made sense. The world works this way. Total free will. If it's going to be, it's up to me. Problem was, it wasn't scriptural and so Pelagius and his teachings were deemed heresy by the early church as works righteousness.

The next theologian, Augustine, taught against Pelagius and said that we are fallen creatures who are unable to make that step. We need help. We need God's grace in order to respond by feeding the hungry, clothing the naked, giving offerings, and praying to God. Augustine seemed to correct the ladder theology of Pelagius by understanding human nature, the bound will and original sin.

Then people began asking the question, "Just how do you get the grace to climb the ladder?" Over time, the church taught that grace was dispensed by the church. The church had the power to grant or withhold that grace. If you paid your money, the church dispensed grace. If you said your prayers and attended worship, the church dispensed grace. If you made a pilgrimage, did a good work, or went to confession, the church dispensed you grace. You can't climb on your own. But grace, doled out by the church, gave you the ability to climb. The more good works, the more you were rewarded with grace. Now it was you, God, and the church climbing up that ladder toward heaven. But it was still a ladder.

Martin Luther grew up with this ladder theology. The picture Luther had of Jesus was a well-known wood carving of his day depicting Jesus holding a lily in one hand and a sword in the other. Heaven and hell. It's your choice. Better start climbing. So Luther spent his days in confession, prayer, worship, and good works because it just made sense that there was no other way to the top but by earning your way step by step.

It makes sense, logically. It should work, theoretically. But what happens when it doesn't work, when I don't feel forgiven, when I'm still racked with guilt, or when I'm not making any progress? What happens when I still sin the same sin, when I feel distant from God despite my most ardent prayers, persistent good works, and generous alms? What happens when it doesn't work?

You either try to climb harder, as Luther did, or blame yourself and end up hating the God you are trying to please. Or you come to the awful conclusion that if it is not my fault, I'm not going up that ladder, then it must be God's fault. Maybe God has said no to me and has rejected me for all of eternity.

It was at the quandary that Luther dove into the teachings of scripture. In Romans 1 he read, "The just shall live by faith." In

Romans 5, "Christ died for our sins while we were still sinners." In John 15, "You did not choose me but I chose you." In our text for today, "All things are lawful for me, but not all things are beneficial." And Luther realized that there was indeed a ladder. But it wasn't one meant for us to climb to heaven. We can't do that. Our rebellious, sinful nature does not seek out a righteous God. Our free will is bound in rebellion against God. It despises God, flees from God, even hates God. So instead of coaxing us up an impossible ladder, God turned the ladder upside down and climbed down to us. We are saved by faith alone in this God who comes to us.

Luther's foes were not so easily persuaded. One Catholic theologian named Erasmus took Luther on head to head precisely over this issue of faith and good works. You may think it strange but Luther actually welcomed this debate against this well-known and intelligent theologian. He actually thanked Erasmus because he alone understood the heart of the issue. This whole Reformation was not about indulgences, not about priests marrying, not about the authority of the pope, not about transubstantiation. The Reformation was a fundamental doctrinal issue about how we get from point A to point B. How do we, fallen, sinful creatures, ever attain to the pinnacle of that ladder? Erasmus said, "Try a little harder, jump a little higher, give a little more, pray more often because your good works will merits God's grace so that together you can climb to the top."

Luther turned the ladder upside down. That's not what the Bible says. "For we hold that a person is justified by faith apart from works of law" (Romans 3:28). And then he drew a line in the sand and said, "Justification by faith through grace is the doctrine upon which the church stands or falls." Erode this and reduce Christianity to a set of morals and the whole thing begins to crumble.

Christianity is not about morality. It's not about climbing a ladder. It's not a partnership between you and God to enable you to get from point A to point B. Do you believe that? Most don't. Most church-going active Christians still believe that to get to heaven, you have to be a good person who climbs ladders. Luther's teachings were not about becoming moral people. Indeed, Luther's warts were uglier, bigger, and more visible than most of ours. His legacy is confessing that he could not climb that ladder. He admitted freely, "I am in bondage to sin and cannot free myself." The gospel doesn't make you a sinless person. The gospel means that those sins are no longer held against you. The sin remains. We are still sinners. Romans 3 says that all have sinned and fallen short of the glory of God. And, at the same time, we are saints who are forgiven for Jesus' sake.

We love ladders. We trust ladders. When we are faced with this grace-filled message of an upside down ladder, we step back, rub our chins and think, "But I have to do something, don't I? I have to participate in this climb, don't I? I at least have to show up, accept, believe, and decide, don't I?" We can either back off and water down the Reformation or we can stand firm with Paul when we writes about the freedom of the Christian in Romans, Galatians, Ephesians, and here again in 1 Corinthians.

But I have to do something, don't I? No, because you can't. There is a rebel living in your heart. This is a one-sided, unilateral act of God's grace, turning the ladder upside down and choosing you, accepting you, believing in you.

"But I have to do something, don't I?" The rebel inside who loves the ladder wants to know. But Paul says here and elsewhere that the answer is, "No. For freedom Christ has set you free. Do not submit again to the yoke of slavery" (Galatians 5:1). We hold that a person is justified by faith apart from works.

Now there is an even better question to ask: "Now that I don't have to do anything, how then shall I live?" Paul says that we are free but then warns, "Do not let your freedom be an opportunity for the flesh." You are free. The ladder is not for you to climb to God but for God in Christ to climb down to you. How then shall you live? Will it be for yourself or will it be a life that is pleasing to God?

Whenever I speak to the middle school youth at church, they want to climb a ladder. They say, "Do I have to go to church? Do I have to go to Sunday school? Do I have to help my neighbor? Do I have to share what's mine? Do I have to pray?"

Do you hear the ladder theology? It is in each one of us.

To answer their questions, I say, "No. You are a Christian. You don't have to, you get to. You get to go to worship to hear that your sins are forgiven. You get to help your neighbor by being the hands of Christ. You get to pray to a God who longs to listen. You don't have to, you get to. That is the freedom you have in Jesus who climbed a ladder down to you."

All things are lawful, but not all things are beneficial. The question is not what you have to do. The question now is what do you get to do for the sake of the kingdom.

Choose wisely! Amen.

Maybe Today

... the appointed time has grown short....
— 1 Corinthians 7:29

Amelia Bedelia is a favorite literary children's character. This poor, dim-witted maid is a literalist. You tell her to dust the tables, and she sprinkles talc everywhere. You tell her to dress the turkey, and she gets out a little lime green pantsuit. You tell her to draw the curtains and she gets out her sketch pad.

In reading about Amelia Bedelia, you realize that we have many phrases that are confusing — especially if you take them literally. "Happy as a clam." Are they really that happy? Or, "I'm so mad I could wring your neck," Come on, we don't mean that ... do we?

The Bible does the same thing. It also uses words, paints pictures, and employs literary devices to convey a truth oftentimes above or beyond the literal words. Now, to be sure, some truths have to be literal or historical in order for them to be true. For example, the person of Jesus is based on a real, live person who actually once walked on this earth. It has to be historically true in order to be true. In the same way, for the resurrection to be true, it has to be historically true. There are some truths that absolutely have to be grounded in fact and history in order to be true.

But there are some truths that do not have to be historical or factual to be true. For example, there is the parable of the good Samaritan where a man went from Jerusalem down to Jericho and was jumped by thieves who left him half dead. If that had never happened historically, that is, if there were no such man who made such a trip, that parable would still be true. Why? Because the truth of that story is not contingent on the historical fact of a man walking down a road but rather in the truth about helping one's neighbors. See the difference?

Another example. Jesus told his disciples that if your right hand causes you to sin, what are you to do? Cut it off. What about your eye? If your eye causes you to sin, what are you to do with it? Pluck it out. Really? If that were literally true, our church would be full of one-eyed, one-handed Christians. But instead, the truth is not contingent on the actual, literal fact. The truth is in the teaching of being constantly wary, always alert to whatever leads you down that path of temptation — and then do all that you can to avoid it.

Same thing when Jesus says, "Take up your cross and follow me." He is not telling all Christians to be literally nailed to a cross and hung up to die. The truth of that phrase is found in the teaching of commitment and self-sacrifice, not in one being crucified.

Got it? The Bible uses many different styles of writings to convey truth. But Christians disagree, at times, as to when to take the words literally and when to seek out the truth above the literal, factual words. This is especially true about words concerning heaven and the return of Jesus. How do you picture heaven? The Bible speaks of heaven in several ways. Streets paved with gold. Is this literal or does it convey a truth of rarity and splendor? There will be wings, halos, and harps. Is this true or does that mean we will have a different existence? Jesus said it is like a mansion where he goes to prepare a place for you. Is there such a place or is Jesus comforting his scared disciples with a reassurance that when that day comes, God will take care of them ... in style?

In 1 Corinthians 7, Paul wrote about the return of Jesus. What will that look like? The *Left Behind* series has painted a vivid picture for its millions of readers. Will it be like that? Isaiah talks about a great banquet, a dessert table with no calories. Is that literally true or does that image convey a truth of intimacy and fellowship? Scripture also talks about being reunited with all the saints but will it be like some big summer family reunion at the lake?

In this text, Paul does not paint a picture for us. Perhaps because it is less important to describe the indescribable and more important to teach about a constant state of readiness. Paul moves beyond the pictorial language and gets very practical with sound advice about marriage, wealth, and emotions. He urges all Christians to be in a constant state of expectation because Paul expected Jesus to return in his lifetime and he lived with that expectation. The gospel authors expected Jesus to return in his lifetime and they lived with that expectation. Luther expected Jesus to return in his lifetime and he lived with that expectation. Mark Allen Powell expects Jesus to return in his lifetime and he lives today, 2,000 years after Paul's words, with that same expectation. Let me tell you about Dr. Powell.

Dr. Powell is a New Testament professor at Trinity Lutheran Seminary. He describes himself as a self-professed Jesus Freak from the 1970s. You know the type? Going to malls and stopping people asking them where they would spend eternity if they were to die that night. Thanking God for everything including getting a great parking spot downtown during lunchtime. They had all the T-shirts, jewelry, and bumper stickers with crosses, fish, and pithy sayings.

Now he is a professor of New Testament teaching our young pastors the truths of the New Testament. Now he knows better. Now he is educated. Now he is enlightened with the truth that rises above the mere literal words. And yet, when that perfect parking spot opens up right in front of the store during rush hour, the first words on his lips are, "Thank you, Jesus." Now, he knows that the God of the universe, the creator of all things, is not holding back cars from blocks around just so he wouldn't have to walk more than fifty feet into the grocery store. He knows that. Besides, there are probably far more people deserving of that spot than he. And yet those words well up from his heart and through his lips. "Thank you, Jesus."

Same with the second coming. "And then they will see the Son of Man coming in a cloud with power and great glory. Now when these things begin to take place, look up and raise your heads, because your redemption is drawing near" (Luke 21:27-28). He has studied the text, he understands the literary genre, he has siphoned off the truth that Luke is trying to convey. He has rationalized this kind of talk as a means by which prescientific people understood the world. It has no literal meaning for today's scientific, educated world.

And yet (and this is the good part), and yet ... every morning when Dr. Powell wakes up, he looks outside up into the sky. If it is one of those clear blue days, that's okay. But if the sky has a couple of those big, puffy clouds, his heart skips a beat and he thinks to himself, "Maybe. Maybe today. Maybe this is the day he's coming."

Do you live with that expectation, do you live with the hope that this could be the day? Which brings up a good question. Paul wrote about Jesus coming back in his lifetime. The gospel authors wrote about Jesus coming back in their lifetimes. Luther wrote about Jesus coming back in his lifetime. Were they wrong? He didn't show up. It's been 2,000 years. Were they all wrong?

Depends. Jesus did not come back during their lifetimes. That much is true. But they all lived with the expectation that he would come back during their lifetime. And for that, they were not wrong.

See the difference? We are called to live with that expectation that this could be the day. But it's tough, isn't it? How long can you stand on your tip toes, stare off the horizon and say, "Any day, soon, hold on, he's coming, I just know it," until the muscles get sore, the eyes grow dim, the voice grows weary and the heart sinks? What does it mean to live your life expecting Jesus' return?

I once read a story by Alvin Rogness, past president of Luther Seminary. When he grew up in South Dakota during the Depression, every spring men would gather in the town on hiring day looking for a farm to work on during the season. On farmer arrived late and found only one guy left standing — a quiet guy without a whole lot to say. But when asked, the hired man said that he was a hard worker and could sleep on a windy night. With no one else to hire, the farmer brought him home.

Everything worked out fine. The farmer had no complaints. Then one night, a tremendous storm ripped across the North Dakotan plain. The wind howled and shook the farm. The farmer ran out to check on the chickens but they were all locked up on the coop. He ran to the barn to latch down the window, but they were all taken care of. He went to find the cattle, but they were all rounded up.

On the way back to the house, he stopped in to check on the hired man who was asleep ... on a windy night.

The truth of the biblical teaching of the second coming of Jesus is not meant to scare you that you might be "left behind," but rather to live your life with expectation so that you are prepared at all times. Some need to make some changes, some are not ready, some can't sleep on a windy night because ... well, because they have left too many things undone and cut to many corners. But others who live with that expectation that this could be the day, see things differently.

I remember one person I visited in the hospital going through a major surgery. He was surrounded by a loving family who were sick with worry, overcome with fear, and stricken with doubt. And instead of ministering to this sick man in the bed, this man of faith was ministering to them, assuring them, "Either way the surgery goes, I'll be okay. I'll be okay."

That's being able to sleep on a windy night. That's living with expectation. Sometimes you have to walk through the valley of the shadow of death to realize that you will be okay.

Oh, I know that the Bible is filled with word pictures and images that may not be literally true — streets of gold, angels with wings, harps, and a pearly gate. I know, I know. I'm too smart for that.

And yet, when that perfect blue sky is dotted with a single white puffy cloud I now think, "Maybe today. Maybe this is the day. I've got a grandpa I want to see again who taught me how to fish. I caught my first northern pike with him on a red and white daredevil on the Mississippi River in Red Wing, Minnesota. Maybe today. Maybe this is the day. Stir up your power, O Lord, and come. 'Cause either way, I'm ready. Either way, I'll be okay." Amen.

The Struggle For Freedom

But you must be careful with this freedom of yours.
— 1 Corinthians 8:9a (NLT)

There is a scene in Tom Hanks' movie, *Forrest Gump*, that came to mind when I read this text in 1 Corinthians. As a young boy, Forrest has to wear these clumsy, heavy leg braces. For the most part, he doesn't care. In fact, the braces become so much a part of his life that he doesn't even realize much how they have trapped and confined him.

And then one day, some bullies chase Forrest and he has to run away but the braces slow him down. As the bullies get closer and closer and Forrest struggles to run faster, the braces finally break, fall off his legs, and suddenly he is set free to run fast.

The point is this, Forrest never knew what it felt to be free or how fast he could run until he took that step or, in a better sense, was forced to break out of braces, and live differently, to live beyond himself. He never went back to the braces.

On the surface, Paul wrote about practical issues. Can we eat meat sacrificed to idols? This is where the freedom of the gospel hit the harsh reality of living in a pagan culture. With his answer, Paul challenged his readers to live a life that is not shaped by the limits of legalism but in the freedom that breaks the shackles of those braces and allows us to live Spirit-filled.

Paul took three missionary journeys throughout Asia Minor. Typically, he would go into a town, plant a church, train leaders, stay for a significant period of time, and then move on to another town and repeat the process elsewhere. However, there was a problem. Only fifteen years after the death of Jesus, there was already a split in Christianity. There were Jewish Christians who thought that Jesus came only for the Jews. As Paul encountered Gentiles, these Jewish/Christians felt that the Gentiles had to first obey all 613 Jewish Laws before becoming true Christians. However, the Gentiles whom Paul reached knew nothing of Judaism. All they knew was the gospel preached by Paul. See the conflict? It comes down to two questions. How am I saved and how must I live? The answer to those two questions depended on whom you asked.

The Jewish/Christian who would come into town after Paul would say, "Yes, you are saved by your faith in Jesus Christ but Paul neglected to tell you the rest of the requirements for becoming one of us." And there were three specific things these Jewish Christians demanded the Gentiles must follow: circumcision, dietary laws, and the observance of holy days.

The book of Galatians is written specifically to this conflict. In Galatians, the issue was circumcision. There were Jewish/Christians who nearly overturned all of Paul's hard work by legalistically demanding circumcision.

In 1 Corinthians, the issue was dietary laws. When Paul was asked in Corinth about eating meat sacrificed to idols he said, "This is not a problem. We know that those idols are made of stone or wood. There is no god there. The sacrifice meant nothing. Pass the steak sauce and eat." There is complete freedom in the gospel to eat meat sacrificed to idols because we are not saved by what we eat or don't eat.

But in that freedom, there are limits. Paul says, "But if eating meat sacrificed to idols causes a weaker or younger person to stumble, question his faith, doubt his integrity, and undermine the unity of the gospel, then he shouldn't eat it."

Is that hypocrisy? No, that's common sense. As an adult, you may choose to drink a glass of wine but if there are youth present at a party who might take your behavior the wrong way, you simply refrain from drinking that night. There are some activities that are inappropriate with mixed company. That's not hypocrisy. That's limiting your freedom for the sake of the other person, particularly the "weaker brethren" as Paul called them.

This is a big deal for Paul. We are saved by faith and not by what we eat or don't eat. In Galatians, Paul says, "For freedom Christ has set you free. Do not submit again to the yoke of slavery." Then he adds, "Only do not let your freedom be an opportunity for the flesh" (Galatians 5:1, 13). In other words, there are limits to our freedom. What are those limits?

In his short book, *Freedom of a Christian*, Luther explained this freedom by saying that a Christian is "a perfectly free lord of all, subject to none ... [and] a perfectly dutiful servant of all, subject to all." Luther used the very teaching of Paul to say that while we are set free from the law through the gospel, the limit to this freedom is summarized in the words of Jesus, Paul and Luther, "The love of the neighbor." That will be what defines us and not the law.

Forrest could have kept those leg braces on his whole life and he wouldn't have known it. All he would know is what he couldn't do. He couldn't run, can't swim, couldn't dance, couldn't play ball, couldn't cross his legs, couldn't put his foot behind his head, or couldn't do yoga. He would spend his life defining himself by what he couldn't do.

There are Christians like that. They define themselves by what they can't do. Can't drink, can't smoke, can't dance, can't play cards, can't watch movies. Oh, we are long past talking about circumcision and dietary laws but the same issue is at stake. Freedom. What am I allowed to do? If I am saved by grace, then am I free to do as I please?

There is an old, subtitled movie called *Babette's Feast*. It is the story of a woman, Babette, who has escaped the French Revolution with nothing but the clothes on her back. She ends up in a very small, parochial Danish village where she is employed by two spinster sisters whose minister father founded the village. The town has no joy. Religious rules are overbearing. Pleasure, music, laughter, and frivolity are vices to be scorned. There is a deep, heavy shroud of weariness blanketing all the people.

Babette is an accomplished chef but is told to prepare each day a thin broth with bread. When she suggests some variation in the meal, she is quickly told that such pleasures are not of God. This is a place defined by what they cannot do.

One day, Babette receives news that she has won the French lottery. The amount of money that she now has will enable her to move from that dreary village and reestablish her life wherever she wants. Faced with all of this freedom, she makes her choice. Babette takes all of her winnings and purchases the most extravagant food from live quails and turtles to unusual spices and seasonings. For the next week, she prepares the most exquisite feast that this village has ever had. And they come. They come hesitantly at first but then through this feast, open up with conversation, laughter, and joy that they have never before experienced.

The only problem is that Babette is once again penniless. She has used her freedom as a servant to her neighbors. But in doing so, she not only set herself free but allowed this small village to taste the true freedom of life in the Spirit.

In 1 Corinthians 8, Paul teaches us that our freedom is a gift given at an incredible price paid by Jesus who gave up his freedom for our sake. Therefore, don't let the guiding force behind your actions be your desires and urges, your boldness and arrogance, or your indulgences and addictions. Let that guiding force be the same as Jesus' — the love of the neighbor. Until you understand your freedom as being a servant to the other person, you will continue to be in bondage.

People sometimes accuse Christians of cheap grace. We have been set free from the law. We fling grace around easily but don't hold people accountable to a high, moral standard. This is a misunderstanding of Paul. In setting us free, the gospel shatters those braces and enables you to live at an even higher level. We live no longer to ourselves but in a life that is pleasing to God through serving the needs of others, particularly the weaker brethren.

Christianity is indeed free but it isn't cheap. It comes with a high price. For how do you make grace expensive? By taking attendance at church? By dictating what you can eat or drink? By handing in your W2s to the church office? By everyone taking their turn at the soup kitchen? By putting cameras in your homes? No. To make grace expensive, you count how many lashes tore his back, you count how many nails pierced his skin, you count how many thorns were in his crown. To make grace expensive, you don't count how much it cost you but how much it cost God to put on this feast for you. That is what makes you free. That's what breaks those braces so that you are free to love your neighbor. Amen.

Witness: More Than Judgment

... I try to find common ground with everyone so that I might bring them to Christ.
— 1 Corinthians 9:22 (NLT)

I have this hobby; well, it's not really a hobby, it's more like a habit, a bad habit. All right, if the truth be known, it's a confession. It's something that I don't share with many people. When I am alone, watching television, and no one is around, I find myself clicking on those obscure channels that feature those down-home preachers. I'm not talking about the large church, multimedia, world-class communicators. I'm talking about the guy with the black toupee with his wife at his side playing the guitar. Or the sweaty guy, wiping his forehead, rocking back and forth, and getting into this frothy, rhyming mantra. Or the one who is going hoarse, scolding the viewers about the best they could hope for was a front seat in hell. Have you ever seen them?

Here's the confession part. I'm not watching them to steal sermons or to learn about delivery or even for personal edification. I watch with some comic disbelief that they think that their message is so good, so powerful, so life-changing that they ought to be on television.

I hear anger in their voices. I hear hell. What I hear is judgment. And I think, "Does this work? Are there those who really stumble across this channel, receive a tongue lashing, and believe?" There has to be a more effective way in reaching people. Think back. Have you experienced someone with good intention witnessing to you

75

but they just ended up doing more damage than good? If we are going to be people who live out faith passionately how do we witness, how do we share that faith in an effective and edifying way that goes beyond frightening images of hell and eternal judgment?

This is important because sharing our faith is not an option. Over 1,500 times in the Bible, it says, "Go." Go to the lost sheep. Go and tell. In Matthew 28 Jesus says, "Go into all the nations and make disciples." Jesus calls us not only to come to him but also to go for him. If you believe and don't go, you had better have a pretty convincing argument as to why you've decided to disobey a pretty blunt and plain command by Jesus to go and speak the gospel to others.

Paul had this urgency about his work. In our epistle for today, he says,

> If I proclaim the gospel, this gives me no ground for boasting, for an obligation is laid on me, and woe to me if I do not proclaim the gospel! For if I do this of my own will, I have a reward; but if not of my own will, I am entrusted with a commission.
>
> — 1 Corinthians 9:16-17

His tactic? It is to be a fellow traveler and pilgrim to walk with people in order to show them the way. He writes,

> To the Jews I became as a Jew, in order to win Jews. To those under the law I became as one under the law (though I myself am not under the law) so that I might win those under the law. To those outside the law I became as one outside the law (though I am not free from God's law but am under Christ's law) so that I might win those outside the law. To the weak I became weak, so that I might win the weak. I have become all things to all people, that I might by all means save some. I do it all for the sake of the gospel, so that I may share in its blessings.
>
> — 1 Corinthians 8:20-23

How do we share the faith? For some, it is through their actions. Some say that our actions speak louder than words — and they are right. Your actions will reveal more about your beliefs than your words. Saint Francis of Assisi said to preach the gospel at all times and if need be, use words. In other words, a righteous life will be noticed by others whereas a phony can be spotted a mile away. A godly life is your proclamation and witness. That's true.

But if all I had to depend on was just my good works, I'd be in trouble. If I thought for a minute that just living out my life, cutting my grass, playing with my children, or shopping at the grocery store would be such a beacon of light unto the whole world that they would see me, be overwhelmed by my actions and convert to Christianity, I'd be in trouble. The gospel would be in trouble. I'm not that good. (And guess what? Neither are you.) I'm glad that I have my words to share. I'm glad I can talk about grace, forgiveness, and mercy when my actions betray the sin within. But how? How do I speak? How do we become a Jew to the Jew or weak for the weak so that more can hear and believe? That's where we all need help.

We have a neighbor who moved in sometime early this summer. It was just before we went on vacation and then school started and the fall race began. You understand how that is. He is right next door and I still haven't had a meaningful conversation with him. And I want to, I want to as a neighbor and I want to as a Christian. But now it has been several months. How long are they still new?

In our home, we have divided up the household chores. My job is to walk to the end of the driveway, open up the mailbox, and bring the mail into the house. (Hey, we all do our part!) In my home, if I don't get the mail, I don't see the mail. My family divides it among themselves and scatters it throughout the house, car, bathroom, and garage. It's like a scavenger hunt to find the bills. So I've told the family that the mail is my job.

One day when I was doing my household chores, I saw my neighbor picking up his mail. We waved, called each other by name, but I have yet to take those thirty steps to his mailbox and have a meaningful conversation that goes beyond the weather. Why? You know why. Dinner's ready. I want to see my family. I've got another appointment. And sometimes, quite frankly, I'm not sure what to say or how to say it or how to raise the religion issue. So

77

I drop the junk mail into the garbage, head into the garage, close the door and think, "I should have said something." I doubt that he sees me cutting my grass, taking out the garbage, and trimming the hedge and is coming to faith because of my righteous yard work. No, I should have said something. I should have taken those thirty steps ... but now he is inside with his family, with his dinner, with his life. Now it's too late.

Who has God placed in your heart? Who is God whispering to you, "Go to them. Take those thirty steps. Talk to them." And you haven't, yet? A neighbor who is either new or has gone through an illness, divorce, or death. A coworker who needs a friend. A family member (these are the most difficult) who is searching for answers while you are silent. I think we all have that person in our life. I think we are even convinced that we ought to share our faith to that person. I don't think that's the issue. The issue is how. How do I do that so I don't sound like a cable free-access preacher? How do I do that authentically, naturally, effectively? How do I have that urgency of Paul to enter into their world and share with them the faith that is in me? Let me give you four very practical pointers that have given me the courage to take those thirty steps.

The first pointer is *purpose*. You've got to be clear in your own heart why you would take those thirty steps. What is the purpose? Some people evangelize like they are pinning scalps to their belt. "I've lead 57 people to the Lord." That's not it. The purpose is that everyone with whom you lock eyes today is someone for whom Jesus died. And if they are worth Jesus dying on the cross, then they are certainly worth walking thirty steps. Let me give you some stats. If our neighborhoods were boiled down to 100 people, 96 would say that they believe in God. That's good. Less than half, 45 people, would have their names on some church or synagogue roster. That's so-so. Of those, 30% would actually go to church. That means of those 100 people, only fifteen would actually be regular worship attenders. Fifteen percent! That's not enough. John wrote his gospel for this reason: "... that you may believe that Jesus is the Christ, the Son of God, and that believing you may have life in his name" (John 20:31). That's the purpose. Faith in Jesus matters for eternity.

The second pointer is *persuasion*. People are smart these days. They go into the doctor's office more knowledgeable about a disease than the doctor. People buy a car today knowing how much the dealer paid for it. You don't have to have a seminary degree but you had better have a good understanding of the basic questions that they will ask. "Why do bad things happen to good people? What happens to the person who never has heard the gospel? How can Jesus be the only way? What do Lutherans, Methodists, Presbyterians believe?" Are you ready? First Peter 3:15 says, "Always be prepared to make a defense to anyone who calls you to account for the hope that is in you." Get resources. Go to classes. Be prepared.

The third pointer is *personal*. Think back to the person who made the biggest spiritual impact on your life. Was it with judgment or with mercy? Finger in your face or arms around your shoulders? Religion or faith? Fear or forgiveness? Hell or heaven? When I think of those people in my life who shaped me most, they were authentic people who didn't have neat, academic answers but struggled with my questions, told me about their doubts, shared with me difficult life lessons learned the hard way and what God taught them about work, family, priorities, failure, death, and guilt. They could identify a turning point in their lives in which their faith was awakened and Jesus became living and real to them. Before you take those thirty steps, you had better know personally the savior about whom you about to speak. It doesn't have to be slick or rehearsed or smooth. It has to come from the heart. Here is where the amateurs always outperform the professional. They will see and believe your heart before they will believe the preacher.

The fourth pointer is *pray*. You might have someone in mind right now that God is putting on your heart. However, if they are not ready to receive the message, you could be Billy Graham and the seed will not grow. Pray for that opportunity. Pray for that divine appointment. When the rich young ruler came up to speak with Jesus and Jesus said, "Go, sell everything that you have and follow me," the man walked away. And Jesus let him. He let him go. Did Jesus fail? No. The man's heart was not ready to receive the message. So pray. Pray for that divine appointment. Pray for that opening.

Pray for the courage to walk thirty steps. Pray for words to speak. And pray for a heart to receive. And don't give up. As a disciple of Jesus, sooner or later, we will all have an opportunity to speak in his name. We are not responsible for what people do with those words. That's the work of the Holy Spirit. But we are responsible for them hearing it.

A staff member of mine, Stephanie, told the story about a neighbor of hers whose young son was killed in a freak boating accident. They had no church. They had no faith. Stephanie wanted to reach out to them but didn't know what to say. Finally, she walked over to their home. It didn't take much. Arms around their shoulders. Tears down everyone cheeks. They were not looking for answers — though they were filled with questions. They were not looking for Stephanie to calm their fears — though they were scared. They were not looking for her to take away all doubt — though they were searching. All they knew was that they were worth taking a walk across the property line. They were worth a knock on the door. They were worth a hug.

After the initial shock, they could hear the gospel for the first time. Do you know how she responded? This neighbor's first response was, "Why haven't I heard this before? Why hasn't anyone told me?" Gulp. Good question. Why not? Telling others about Jesus is the greatest thing you can do for them. It has eternal significance. Your job doesn't. Your schedule doesn't. Your mail doesn't. But Jesus does. Why hadn't she heard it before? Folks, I don't want my neighbor asking God that question — because I know the answer. They cannot be told unless someone decides that if this person is worth Jesus dying for, he is certainly worth me walking thirty steps for. Amen.

Busy With A Purpose

... I do not run aimlessly, nor do I box as though beating
the air. — 1 Corinthians 9:26

We are too busy. A recent CNN Poll found out that 59% of the people felt overcommitted, overbusy, overstressed. In the past ten years, we have somehow lost eight-and-a-half hours a week of free time. I know that's true for me. I know I like a full plate. I like a busy schedule. Therefore, it is difficult for me to talk about slowing down. I needed help putting this message together. So I called several people this past week who are busy people and asked them, "How do you know that you are too busy? What are some of the red flags?" Here they are. This is a self-test. Just check the ones that apply to you.

1. I am home on a Tuesday night and nothing is on the calendar — and I get anxious.
2. I take business reading material with me — to the bathroom.
3. I'm just not fun to be with. I get selfish and demanding. I turn into a task driver. I don't feel well, my head aches, my neck hurts, and I'm tired.
4. I drink coffee all day and switch to wine at 5 p.m. (Some of you are thinking, "Is that bad?")
5. I use my day off to catch up on my work.
6. I have to get sick to take a day off — and I still feel guilty.
7. When I check out at the grocery store, I first calculate

which lane will go fastest by factoring in the number of carts, number of items and the competency of the clerk. Then I keep track of the lane I didn't choose.

8. The family calendar has replaced the family Bible for nightly reading. "Okay, children, open up your calendars to April 29 and let's read together."

9. Everything seems shallow — family, relationships, God. I'm not in the moment. I'm just going through the motions until the next activity.

10. I finally convince myself that something has to give. And you know what? That something usually is the wrong thing. It's my marriage, the kids, church, God, or my health.

It's not that we are doing the bad things. We are busy with church and school activities, community service, music lessons, and academics. All good things in themselves, but when combined together with a family of four or five members, it's crazy. Something has to give.

What is the answer? I don't think the answer is that we all move to the country, grow vegetables, raise goats, start a compost pile, and sell hemp necklaces at the county fair. There has to be something in between going 100 mph and Green Acres. But what?

In 1 Corinthians 9, Paul uses a sport imagery to talk about being busy with a purpose.

> *Do you not know that in a race the runners all compete, but only one receives the prize? Run in such a way that you may win it. So I do not run aimlessly, nor do I box as though beating the air.*
>
> — 1 Corinthians 9:24, 26

There is a purpose to Paul's busyness.

There is an African proverb that says that each morning at dawn in the Serengeti, the gazelle must wake up running because he must run faster than the fastest lion in order to survive. On the same morning in the same Serengeti, the lion must wake up at dawn

running in order to catch the slowest gazelle in order to survive. Both are running, both are very busy, but they know why they run. Do you?

Paul is not saying that running is the problem nor is it being too busy. It is running aimlessly that is the problem. I bet as we scurry from activity to commitment to tournaments, much of our running is aimless.

A couple of years ago, Quaker Oats ran a commercial for their new instant cinnamon cereal. The television shot showed a mother in the kitchen near the microwave talking about how breakfast had really become a chore. She wanted her son to have a healthy breakfast but it would take a long time to make the cereal and then she would have to sit down with little Johnny, talk with him, and coax him to eat. And then the bell of the microwave went off. Now, she said, with this new instant, great tasting breakfast cereal, he gobbles down the cereal in five minutes and we are out the door, not wasting time. And I thought, sitting down to have breakfast with your son is not wasted time. If you think it is, you are running, all right, you are busy, to be sure. But it is aimless.

The key word in 1 Corinthians 9 is "aimlessly." Paul wants to stop us in our calendar tracks, forcing us to reevaluate our schedules, and determine what activities are worthwhile and what is simply aimless. To determine which is which requires some intentional quiet time.

I remember hearing about an interview that Matt Lauer of the *Today* show did with Mother Teresa. He asked her about a typical day. Mother Teresa told Matt that she gets up early and usually spends two hours in prayer and meditation. "Two hours," he said. "What do you do for two hours?" She said, "I listen to God." "And what does God say to you?" Mother Teresa said, "He doesn't speak. He is listening to me." And with that, this world-class interviewer was speechless — not sure if it was awe or confusion. So he broke for a commercial.

The psalmist wrote, "Be still, and know that I am God" (Psalm 46:10a). Certainly there is a time to make your request known to God with great details. Certainly there is a time to sing at the top of your lungs. Certainly, there is time to be busy, doing the work of the Lord, but there is also a time to be still. In Mark, the evangelist wrote, "In the morning, while it was still very dark, [Jesus] got up and went out to a deserted place, and there he prayed" (Mark 1:35). Jesus was a very busy man but he was not running aimlessly. To keep centered, he needed to be still.

There is an off button to the phone, the computer, the palm pilot, the radio. Use it. We are a loud society. Be still in order to listen and to be heard so that you are not boxing by beating the air.

James Dobson of *Focus on the Family* was talking once about focusing our lives on what is truly important. He told a story about his college days when his whole life was consumed by tennis. He spent time training, practicing, and playing tennis until he won the championship and received a large trophy for first place, a trophy that was proudly displayed in the sports hall of fame at the school.

And then one day, several years later, he received a package in the mail from his alma mater. Inside was his trophy and a handwritten note. "I found this in the trash at school as they were cleaning out the trophy cases. I thought you might like this."

All those accomplishments that we think are so important will one day be forgotten. Trophies that define us and plaques that identify us will crumble like dust. Paul makes it clear that he doesn't want that to happen to his life. He wants his life to count. He longs for meaning and purpose, not running aimlessly or beating the air.

Jesus asked, "What does it profit a person to gain the whole world and forfeit his soul?" (Mark 8:36). Let's change that a bit and ask, "What does it profit a person to gain the whole world, win the entire tournament, close the biggest deal, have the busiest calendar, and forfeit his marriage, his children, his health, and his God?"

I don't think the answer to our jammed calendars is doing nothing but something has to give, right? What will that something be — marriage, children, health, or God? Or will it be something else?

Obviously, this cannot be fixed with one sermon, but we can take a step in the right direction. What is one thing in your life right now that has to give?

Something that is taking up so much time that you feel as if you cannot be still.

Something that feels like busy work, makes you run aimlessly and beating the air.

Something that you've turned to instead of God for a sense of worth, value, and importance.

Being busy is not the problem. Running at full steam is not the problem. Running without a purpose is. Decide right now what's gotta give before the wrong thing gives. Amen.

Integrity: Words With Meaning

My yes means yes. — 2 Corinthians 1:18b (NLT)

Integrity means that your words have meaning. Paul writes, "... am I like people of the world who say yes when they really mean no? As surely as God is true, I am not that sort of person. My yes means yes" (2 Corinthians 1:17-18b NLT).

That is extremely important today because more and more we are surrounded by meaningless words. You can't turn on the radio without an announcer yelling at you that there has never been a better time to buy a car. Infomercials have products that if you act now, they will throw in an additional dicer and mincer at no extra charge. I heard a story of meaningless words about a high-level executive who traveled weekly for his job. Every Monday morning he went through the same routine. He arrived at the airport early, picked up his *Wall Street Journal*, sipped his Starbucks coffee, boarded the plane in first class, and waited for his breakfast to be served. On one occasion, as he was glancing at the headlines, he lifted the cover off his bagel and saw this huge, ugly roach upside down on his bagel, legs still twitching.

He came unglued. Not only did the flight attendant hear about it, but the entire airplane could not help but overhear his ranting about the roach. He demanded the name of the flight attendant and the pilot and the caterer and their next of kin. As soon as he got to his first-class hotel, he wrote a letter on his impressive stationary to the president of the airline, issuing his complaint.

To his satisfaction, he received a prompt letter back from the president of the airline. It read: "I am terribly sorry about your unfortunate incident on our airplane. I take full responsibility. We have canceled our contract with the meal service, fired the flight attendant and the staff, removed all the upholstery, and fumigated the entire plane. It will be out of service for the next nine months. I hope this is acceptable to you and that you will consider flying with us again. Signed ..."

The executive felt pretty good about himself and the fear he caused in the airline until he noticed a sticky note absentmindedly left on the back of the letter from some secretary. It was from the president's assistant and read, "Send this guy the roach letter!"

Meaningless words. Every day we need to sift through the muck and mire of empty words to find some real substance, integrity, and truth. Faced with this same uncertainty, Paul had to defend his decisions in 2 Corinthians 1 by claiming that he was a man of his word because of the integrity found in being a follower of Jesus.

I have a friend named Susie who told me the story of growing up as a pastor's child. While there was always lots of love, there was not always a lot of extras. When they went to the movies, it was a real treat.

She remembered one time going to a movie with only her father. Susie has always been a small person — especially as a young teen. When they got to the ticket booth, her father said, "Two adults, please." The lady behind the counter said, "How old is your daughter?" "Thirteen," he said. "Oh, she looks twelve. I'll just charge you for the child's price. Nobody will know." Reaching for his wallet, her dad said, "She'll know," and he put down money for two adult tickets.

Do your words, do your actions have integrity or are you part of the noise and chatter of meaningless words? Does your yes mean yes and your no mean no?

What about in your business? Do your words have integrity? I remember hearing a story about the boardroom in which the CEO felt the company had lost its focus. So, as an illustration, he wrote on the whiteboard, "2 + 2," and asked the entire board, "Let's get down to basics once again. What is two plus two?"

There was a mathematician on the committee who said, "The answer is 4." The vice president of marketing said, "I agree. The answer is 4, give or take a margin of error of 1 point." However, the CPA silently got up, shut the door, pulled the shade, and whispered, "What do you want it to equal?"

Can God trust you when you are alone with the door closed and shades pulled? Integrity means that you are the same person in or outside the spotlight, with or without the cameras running, standing alone or in front of the audience. Integrity doesn't mean perfection. Integrity means authenticity, consistency, and an undivided life. Do your words and your actions have meaning? Are you a person of your word? George Burns once said, "The most important thing in acting is honesty. If you can fake that, you've got it made."

The people of Corinth were watching Paul. If he could be trusted, then his message could be trusted. We in the church are being watched, also. People can sniff out a fraud. They want to know if you are a person of integrity.

I heard a pastor tell the story of a hectic and busy day. It was one of those days that had to be divided into fifteen-minute segments for it all to fit. As he went from meeting to meeting, visit to visit, he actually found himself ahead of schedule by thirty minutes. It was then he saw it. It was a music store that advertised CDs on sale at half price. Knowing he couldn't pass up such a bargain, he checked his watch, parked his car, and ran into the store.

He didn't have much time. He grabbed the CD he wanted, hurried to the counter, gave the young lady the CD and his credit card, quickly signed the receipt, and ran back to the car. Back on time. With any luck, he could make it to the next meeting.

It was then he glanced at the receipt for the first time. Instead of charging him $6.99 for the CD, the clerk charged him 69 cents. Now what? For a moment he thought about letting it go. No one would know the difference. Then he glanced at his watch, grabbed the receipt, and ran back into the store.

He quickly found the clerk, showed her the receipt, and told her that there had been a mistake. The young woman was speechless. The pastor didn't quite know what to think of it. Then she spoke. "You don't know me but I visited your church last Sunday. I sat in the back row. It has been a long time since I've been to church. I couldn't take all the hypocrisy. And then I heard you talk about integrity from the pulpit. When I saw you come in here, I wanted to see if you really meant it or if you were just one more religious phony. You actually believe this stuff, don't you?"

And with that, the clerk excused herself from the till and sat down with the pastor to tell him more. Not once did he even glance at his watch.

The people of Corinth were watching Paul. The people in your neighborhood and at work are watching you. In a world of meaningless words, in business where two plus two equals whatever you want it to equal, in politics where the spin is endless, in the home and church where we often live behind a cheap facade, you represent Jesus. If you can be trusted, then he can be trusted. If your yes means yes and your no means no, the same is true about Jesus. So when they hear that Jesus forgives sins, promises them a new life, and prepares a place for them for all eternity, they figure his words have meaning, his words have integrity. They may not know Jesus, not yet, but they know you. Amen.

Who Will Vouch For Me?

Surely we do not need, as some do, letters of recommendation to you or from you, do we?
— 2 Corinthians 3:1

William Barkley points out in his commentary on this passage that there was a common practice in the ancient world of sending letters of commendations with a person when he traveled into strange and foreign communities. To insure his reputation or even safety, these letters written by a trusted friend would testify to his character. It was sometimes difficult, however, to determine whether a recommendation was sincere or merely flattery or, worse, forgery.

The same is true today, isn't it? If we don't know someone, we look for a recommendation. There is a true story recorded in the popular book, *Chicken Soup for the Soul.* It is a story about a man who wrote a letter to a small hotel in the Midwest. He planned to stay there during his vacation and wrote the owner this letter. "I would very much like to bring my dog with me. He is well-groomed and very well-behaved. Would you be willing to permit me to keep him in my room with me at night?"

An immediate reply came back from the hotel owner who wrote, "I've been operating this hotel for many, many years. In all that time, I've never had a dog steal towels, bed clothes, silverware, or a picture off the wall. I've never had to evict a dog in the middle of the night for being drunk and disorderly. And I've never had a dog run out on a hotel bill. Yes, indeed, your dog is welcome at my hotel. And, if your dog is willing to vouch for you, you are welcome to stay here, too."

What a surprise. Here the man assumed all along that the dog was the problem and that he would have to vouch for the dog. What a turn of events to find out that the dog was fine. There was nothing wrong with the dog. It was just the opposite. The man was the problem. He was the one needing someone to vouch for him. Who would have guessed it?

There was once a contest to write an essay titled, "What is the Problem with the World?" And there were many submissions that wrote about hunger, war, pollution, greed, racism, and sexism. But the winning essay describing the problem with the world was actually the shortest. Just two words. "I am."

It's true, you know. From the first chapters of Genesis, God reveals the problem with this world. It would be easy to point the finger at all sorts of problems from society to greed to being bottle-fed as a child. But the Bible clearly points the finger where it is due. What's the problem with the world? I am. And if this is true, then who will vouch for me?

Years ago, Notre Dame dominated national college football. The team was led by coach Knute Rockne, known as the Rock, perhaps the most inspirational football coach of all time. In a game defending its title, Notre Dame kicked off to Carnegie Tech who proved to sustain an unstoppable drive. Six yards, ten yards, five yards. Notre Dame was caught backpedaling against the highly spirited Tech team.

But one thing Notre Dame had on its side, or rather its sidelines, was a coach who never gave up, who inspired his team to victory; a coach with all the right strategic calls. The players were convinced that Rock would figure out a way to stop Tech. In the meantime, the ball kept advancing.

When the ball reached the fifty-yard line, the defense looked anxiously toward the sidelines. What should we do? When Tech reached the thirty-yard line, Rockne grabbed a substitute and barked out commands ... but held him back for a few more plays.

Finally, when Tech reached the three-yard line, Rockne called time out and the substitute came running in from the sidelines with the message.

The defense quickly gathered around the player, absolutely quiet, ready for their instructions, "What should we do?"

The substitute answered, "Rock says, 'For God's sake, hold 'em!'"

That's it! "Hold 'em." It's up to you. For in the end, we are the one held accountable. Nowhere is that more evident than when you are struggling on the third-yard line against great odds.

We are the ones accountable. There is no letter of recommendation that can take us off the hook. We would prefer to play the victim, make excuses, exonerate ourselves, hide behind the fluff but really in the last analysis, we need to make an account of our lives — and when we do, we stand alone. When that moment comes, who will vouch for me? When that final breath is taken and I am held accountable for my life ... for what I have done and left undone, for the people I've harmed and the poor I've neglected, who will stand up and vouch for me?

It is here that Paul provides the answer. Our confidence is not in a letter of recommendation or some righteous life that we have lived. Our confidence is not based on our competency or following the letter of the law. Paul says that the law kills but the Spirit gives life. When we finally stand before the throne of God, desperately looking around, our confidence will come from the one who will step forward and say, "It's okay. He's with me. His debt is paid in full. He is blameless. I can vouch for him."

This great gift of forgiveness and grace comes with it a tremendous amount of responsibility. As forgiven believers with letters of recommendation written upon our hearts, we now become Christ's epistles to the world. He has vouched for you. Can you vouch for him?

Pastor and author, Lee Strobel, told the story of a young woman in his church who, after a long time away, finally returned. She had been badly hurt as a child by the so-called Christians in her church that for her to darken the doors again took great courage. She was filled with skepticism and doubt. The walls were high. The scrutiny was tight. As she felt that faith welling up inside her again, she had to make sure it was real. So she wrote Strobel this letter.

Dear Pastor,

Do you know, do you understand that you represent Jesus to me?

Do you know, do you understand that when you treat me with gentleness, it raises the question in my mind that maybe he is gentle, too. Maybe he isn't someone who laughs when I am hurt.

Do you know, do you understand that when you listen to my questions and you don't laugh, I think, "What if Jesus is interested in me, too?"

Do you know, do you understand that when I hear you talk about arguments and conflicts and scars from your past, I think, "Maybe I am just a regular person instead of a bad, no good little girl who deserves abuse."

If YOU care, I think maybe he cares ... and then there's this flame of hope that burns inside of me and for a while I am afraid to breathe because it might go out.

Do you know, do you understand that your words are his words? Your face, his face to someone like me?

Please be who you say you are. Please God don't let this be another trick. Please let this be real. Please.

Do you know, do you understand that you represent Jesus to me?[1]

It is an awesome responsibility, isn't it, to vouch for Jesus? And it won't be done with fading ink or empty words. It can only be done through the heart that has been renewed, restored, and forgiven. He has vouched for you. The Spirit has given you life. Now, vouch for him for the one who longs to know whether or not he is real. Amen.

---

1. Leo Strobel, "Maggie's Poem," *God's Outrageous Claims: Discovering What They Mean for You* (Grand Rapids, Michigan: Zondervan, 2005).

The Transfiguration Of Our Lord
(Last Sunday After Epiphany)
2 Corinthians 4:3-6

The Eyes Of Faith

The god of this world has blinded the minds of the unbelievers, to keep them from seeing the light of the gospel of the glory of Christ, who is the image of God.
— 2 Corinthians 4:4

When you come face to face with some huge obstacle, some daunting problem, something frightening in which the odds are stacked against you, what is your first step? Do you go around it? We learned that as a kid walking home, didn't we? If there were a big, mean dog on the route, we would walk blocks around it to get home safely. How about now? Do you still walk around those big, mean dogs?

Some people go over them. That is, you know the problem is there but you just scratch the surface, gloss over the problem, brush up against it but don't really address it. It's just always there and you minimize the danger. "It's no big deal. I'm fine."

Some people decide to go under it. They bury their heads into the ground and don't even acknowledge it, don't even name it. "If I don't talk about it, maybe it will just go away." But pretty soon the problem suffocates you with its weight.

People with eyes of faith go through it. They can see what others cannot see. They name the problem, identify the problem, stare that problem right in the eye, and decide that the only way to conquer this problem and to get to the other side is to go through it.

95

On this Transfiguration Sunday, the three disciples' eyes were opened. They saw what others could not see. There on the mountaintop, they saw Jesus in all of his glory. Even though they stumbled and were often filled with doubt, they now had eyes of faith.

In the epistle reading today from 2 Corinthians 4, Paul wrote about such eyes of faith. "[The gospel] is veiled only to those who are perishing. In their case, the god of this world has blinded the minds of the unbelievers, to keep them from seeing the light of the gospel of the glory of Christ ..." (vv. 3-4). Paul, however, has eyes of faith. He can see things that others cannot.

Remember the story in 2 Kings about Elisha? The king of Aram was an enemy of Israel. However, he couldn't seem to surprise Israel's army. Unknown to him, God would tell Elisha the prophet where the enemy was lying in ambush and Elisha would warn the king of Israel. Each time, the army of Israel would escape unharmed.

When the king of Aram heard that Elisha was giving away his location time and again, he sent his troop to capture Elisha. They snuck out at night and circled the village. That morning, when Elisha and his servant awoke, they looked outside and each saw an entirely different scene.

The servant saw the soldiers of Aram surrounding them on all sides. He saw defeat. He saw no escape. But Elisha, with eyes of faith, saw something else. And he prayed that God would open his servant's eyes, too. At that very moment, the servant looked up a second time and surrounding the Aramean army was a band of angels who far outnumbered the enemy. Elisha didn't hide, run away, or deceive the enemy. He didn't go around the problem, over the problem, or under the problem. He went through the problem. He faced the problem with eyes of faith knowing in his heart that there were more who were for him than against him.

What are these eyes of faith that the unbeliever does not have? For a long time, I thought about faith in terms of a list of doctrines or beliefs that you have to accept before becoming a part of the club or joining a church. But more recently, I've come to see faith in much more active terms. There are a lot of people who believe in God but don't have faith. Do you understand the difference? You can believe in God without having faith. Faith is living against the odds. Faith has less to do with what you believe and more to do with how you decide to live. Faith is seeing the enemy surround you, the problem overtake you, the crisis overwhelm you, and instead of going around it or over it or under it, you decide to do what Paul and Elisha did — go through it with eyes of faith.

Why's that so important? Because Paul wrote about two ways to live. You can live with blinded eyes that are veiled and are unable to see the glory of God. Or you can live with eyes of faith that walk you through the storms of life. Let me explain that.

Sometimes God parts the water and you walk right through the obstacle. Sometimes he touches the eyes and sight comes back. Sometimes he lifts you up on chariots of fire so you don't have to taste the stench of death. Sometimes God heals miraculously! Unfortunately, those are the exceptions. Usually (and don't ask me why), usually you can't get over or around or under such problems. Most of the time you have to go through them. For that, you need eyes of faith.

Hebrews 11 teaches about this journey through problems. The author describes faith this way: Faith is the assurance of things hoped for, the conviction of things not seen. The only way to see things not seen is through eyes of faith. What does this mean? The author gives some examples.

By faith, we understand that the world was formed by God. We never saw it. By faith, Noah built an ark without ever seeing the first drop of water. By faith, Abraham and Sarah left their homeland not seeing where that journey would take them. By faith, Abraham and Sarah believed they would have a son — not seeing any way that was possible. By faith, Abraham was ready to sacrifice his son not seeing another way out. By faith, Isaac and Jacob blessed their sons not seeing the promise. By faith, Joseph saved his people in Egypt from famine, not seeing the hand of God. By faith, Moses led the people out of bondage in Egypt, through the desert and to the promised land seeing only sand.

And then the authors, after this long list of people who by faith went through these problems with eyes of faith, not seeing how the story will end, concludes with these words:

*By faith these people **overthrew** kingdoms, **ruled** with justice, and **received** what God had promised them. They **shut** the mouths of lions, **quenched** the flames of fire and **escaped** death by the edge of the sword. Their weakness was turned to strength. They became strong in battle and put whole armies to flight.*
— Hebrews 11:33-34 (NLT, emphasis mine)

Look at those active verbs again. They overthrew kingdoms, ruled with justice, shut the mouths of lions, quenched the flames of fire, and escaped death by the sword through faith. I suppose they could have responded differently. I suppose Abraham and Sarah could have run away from the problem and just said, "No, we are not moving." I suppose Noah could have gone around the problem, built a couple of canoes, and hoped for the best. I suppose Joseph could have gone over the problem and shrugged, "Why is a famine that will kill the Egyptians my problem?" I suppose Moses could have gone under the problem and been crushed by the thought of going to the Pharaoh and asking him to release the hundreds of thousands of slaves that they had held in bondage for 450 years.

But instead, they went through with eyes of faith. They could not see where the path would lead or how the story would end but still going through. Sometimes scarred, sometimes beaten, sometimes lonely, but still through seeing what Elisha once saw, "It looks bad out there. The path looks incredibly hard. And no doubt my life is going to get a whole lot worse before it gets better but I press on, I go forward, I go through convinced that there are more who are for me than who are against me."

I remember talking with a person who suffered unspeakable abuse as a child. For a long time he went over it by denying it happened. He tried going around it by avoiding the problem with alcohol, work, and exercise addiction. He tried going under it by shrugging his shoulders and saying, "It happened a long time ago. No big deal." However, the demons of his past were still there, breaking apart his marriage, ruining his business, destroying his health. He realized that he had to strap on the helmet, put on the armor, and go directly through it in battle.

I spoke with him halfway through the battle. He told me he was making progress but then admitted that before it gets any better, it's going to get a whole lot worse. But now, with eyes of faith, he was no longer perishing. He could see the glory of Christ working in him even as he walked through this dark and difficult path. For the first time, he could see that those who were for him far outnumbered those who were against him.

The Bible passage that brought him comfort during this journey was from Isaiah 43.

> ... *Do not be afraid, for I have ransomed you. I have called you by name; you are mine. When you go **through** deep waters and great trouble, I will be with you. When you go **through** rivers of difficulty, you will not drown. When you walk **through** the fire of oppression, you will not be burned up; the flames will not consume you. For I am the Lord your God, the Holy One of Israel, your Savior.* — Isaiah 43:1-3a (NLT, emphasis mine)

Notice the word "through." You will still go through the deep waters. You will still go through the difficult rivers. You will still go through the fire. The difference now is that you do not travel alone. The ones for you far outnumber the ones against you. The difference now is that you have eyes of faith.

How can God say this? Because he doesn't just talk a good line, he has lived it. In the Garden of Gethsemane, Jesus was looking for every way around and over and under this looming cross. He knew the path was difficult. He knew that it was going to get a whole lot worse before it got better. And I suppose even he knew, even as he asked for a way out, he knew that there was only one way he could go — through the cross, through the suffering, and through the agony.

It is this journey with eyes of faith through life's difficult storms that Paul gives this word of hope, "For God who said, 'Let there be light in the darkness,' has made us understand that this light is the brightness of the glory of God that is seen in the face of Jesus Christ" (2 Corinthians 4:6 NLT). Amen.